Strange-But-True Devotions to Jump-Start Your Day

JUMPER FABLES

KEN DAVIS &
DAVE LAMBERT

ZondervanPublishingHouse
Grand Rapids, Michigan

A Division of HarperCollinsPublishers

Jumper Fables

Copyright © 1994 by Ken Davis and David Lambert.
All rights reserved

Requests for information should be addressed to:
Zondervan Publishing House, Grand Rapids, Michigan 49530

Library of Congress Cataloging-in-Publication Data

Davis, Ken, 1946-
     Jumper fables: strange-but-true devotions to jump-start your
faith/Ken Davis and David Lambert
     p. cm.
     ISBN 0-310-40010-4 (paper)
     1. Teenagers–Prayer-books and devotions–English. 2. Teenagers–
Religious life. [1. Prayer books and devotions. 2. Christian
life.] I. Lambert, David (David Wesley), 1948- . II. Title.
BV4850.D37 1993.
242'.63–dc20   93-2113
                                                                        CIP
                                                                         AC

Edited by Mary McCormick

Interior design by Jamison•Bell Advertising & Design

Illustrations by Rand Kruback

Cover design by Paz Design

     94 95 96 97 98 /DH/ 7 6 5 4 3 2 1

For the eight kids who've lived
many of the stories in this book—
and who know that their dads
aren't as smart as they think they are—

Ken's:

Traci and Taryn

and Dave's:

Seth, Sarai, Bryan, Anna, Eric, and Beth

INTRODUCTION

Welcome to *Jumper Fables!* We hope you'll really enjoy this book. But remember that *Jumper Fables* isn't intended to replace or substitute for your reading of the Bible. In fact, using this book as your sole means of spiritual nourishment would be like trying to live on the residue left on candy wrappers—it tastes good but just doesn't meet your minimum daily requirements.

Jumper Fables is designed to be fun, to keep you thinking about issues you face every day, and to stimulate your interest in getting to know God better by studying his Word. You can use the book any way that seems helpful to you, but we wrote it with the idea that you'd read one short section a day. If you do that, and if you read it in the morning, you'll find (we hope!) that it helps you get the day off to a good, positive start—especially if, besides reading *Jumper Fables*, you read the Bible passages we suggest.

Oh—one more thing. This book was written from start to finish by both of us; we both worked on every single daily reading. But most of the stories in the book are Ken's. So most of the time, when you see an "I," that "I" is Ken talking. When you see Dave's name after a title, that means the story is Dave's and the "I" in the story is Dave talking. Got that?

So dig in—and have a good time!

IF IT SQUEAKS LIKE A RAT, IT'S A RAT

A few years ago, I took my family into a restaurant. As we sat down, a surly waitress with the disposition of a linebacker who's just had his head stepped on threw our menus on the table and demanded, "What do you want?" She took our orders without smiling once.

It was as if we were being punished for coming into the restaurant! My mission was clear: I was going to get a chuckle—or at least a little smile—out of that waitress before we left the restaurant. I was a comedian, wasn't I?

In my pocket I had just the tool to do it: a little puppet made out of rabbit fur. Properly manipulated and accompanied by the appropriate squeaks, it looked so much like a rat that I could almost fool myself. After she'd brought our orders and stomped away, I hid that little rascal beneath my salad and hung its leather tail over the edge of the bowl. Then I called her back over. "Oh, Mi—iss!"

She stormed back, scowling. I waited until she stood towering over me, yelling "What?"—then I grabbed the puppet's tail and made that furry little critter run screeching up my arm and down my shirt.

My expectations were modest. I thought I'd get at least a grunt of appreciation out of her. Her response went beyond my wildest dreams. She screamed and backpedaled away from the table, arms flailing, knocking over chairs, and sending ketchup bottles, plates full of food, and napkin dispensers flying in all directions. Then she turned and fled the room at top speed, destroying any table in her path.

I hadn't really intended to scare her; I just wanted to brighten her day. Likewise, I'm sure that when we came in, the management had no intention of kicking us out before we'd even eaten our meal, but that's what they did, shouting threats to call the police if we didn't leave immediately. Ever since then, my wife and kids check my pockets before we enter a restaurant.

It's easy to shake our heads at that waitress's gullibility and say, "But it wasn't even a real rat!" True. But she *thought* it was a real rat. She wasn't running through the restaurant, scattering veal cutlets and hapless patrons, yelling "Fake rat! Fake rat!" To her, it *was* real. And that's the point: It isn't necessarily reality that shapes our behavior and our attitudes—it's what we *believe* about reality.

There's a current TV commercial in which a sexy tennis star says, "Image is everything." Wrong. It's not how we appear to the world but rather, *how we see the world* that is everything. We can see the world from an earthly point of view—sin is inevitable, so we might as well give in; God isn't real; we're weak and stupid; money and status and beauty are everything; it's the present that matters, so live it up.

Or we can see it from God's point of view: This earthly life is just a proving ground for our eternal life; it's what's done for God that really matters; sin is tempting, but with God's help we can resist it. It's what we do for others—not for ourselves—that really counts. We are beloved by God and have an important role to fulfill in life. We matter to God.

How do we learn to see the world in that way? By reading God's Word, the Bible. Read it daily—and learn to see the world as God does. It will change your life. Best of all, you won't find yourself running from fake rats.

VERSE OF THE DAY:

Do good to your servant
according to your word, O Lord.
Teach me knowledge and good judgment.

—Psalm 119: 65, 66

HEY!

Want to see why the Word of God was so important to David the Psalmist? Read Psalm 119:89-93.

JUST DO IT:

Have you ever read the Bible all the way through? I know, it sounds like a huge task. And it is. But if you plan to do it over a whole year, you only have to read a few chapters a day. There are several plans available to do that, some of them with little checklists so that you can check off the chapters after you've read them. If you have *The Student Bible* (Grand Rapids, Michigan: Zondervan Publishing House, 1981), you'll find a reading plan near the front. If you don't, ask your youth pastor or pastor to recommend a reading plan. And be sure to keep it up every day! It'll help you to spot the fake rats and to zero in on reality.

Imagine a football coach's giving his team this pep talk: "Okay, boys—we haven't got a chance today. The other team is against us, and they're a lot better than we are. The officials favor our opponents, and they're near-sighted anyway. So there's not much we can do—just go out there and try to keep the other team from scoring. Try not to get hurt, but if you feel any pain, just quit."

That team would never win a game. To win, you have to have a positive attitude; you have to want to move the ball forward. In the 1987 Western Division playoffs, the Denver Broncos were playing the Cleveland Browns for the championship. It was a very physical game, and the score was 20 to 13 in favor of Cleveland with five minutes left in the fourth quarter. After a muffed kick-off return, Denver ended up with the ball on their own 1 ½-yard line. They had 98 ½ yards to go in five minutes to tie the game and gain a chance to win in overtime. As they huddled, facing what seemed like an impossible position, Keith Bishop turned to his teammates and said, "Okay, boys, now we've got 'em right where we want 'em. If everybody does his job, good things will happen."

Now *that's* a positive attitude. Can you guess what happened? Denver moved the ball all the way down the field, scored a touchdown, and won in overtime.

Can *you* develop that kind of positive attitude? Yes, you can—and God can help. Remember these two principles: First, *have a positive concept of yourself.*

Don't see yourself as a helpless child in a hopeless situation. See yourself as a giant-killer! You were created by a mighty God to accomplish what no one else on earth can accomplish, and he gives you every ounce of power you'll need for the job. You're not a helpless child—you're the child of a king! Because of him, you can accomplish the impossible.

Second, *think positively about the future.* It can be better than the past, better than the present—it's at least partly up to you.

Don't be satisfied with the status quo, and don't make the mistake of assuming the worst. I met someone the other day who called that "awfulizing" (sitting around thinking about the worst that can happen and then assuming it will).

Instead, think of what you *want* to happen and then figure out what you need to do to *make* it happen. Be aggressive!

No matter how difficult things are in your life, look at those challenges the way David looked at Goliath: as an opportunity—for slingshot practice.

VERSE OF THE DAY:

In all these things we are more than conquerors through him who loved us.
—*Romans 8:37*

HEY!

Here's one of my favorite passages in the whole Bible—and it's all about thinking positively: Philippians 4:4-8.

JUST DO IT:

It's one thing to *say* we're going to have a more positive attitude; it's another thing to do something about it. Identify your areas of negativity, especially in the two areas identified above. Now comes the hard part: Decide how you're going to replace those negative attitudes with positive ones. (Hint: Prayer helps. And if you haven't read Philippians 4:4-8 yet, do it now.) Write down the steps you're going to take.

BE A DIAMOND

I spoke not long ago at a Christian youth event where two well-known Christian musical acts were performing during the same evening. These Christian musicians were celebrities to the adoring fans who owned their albums and who had paid to come hear them perform. When the concert was over, those fans rushed the stage for autographs, and the band members came to the front of the stage to sign them. At one end of the stage, a young performer's actions, words, and facial expressions made it clear that he felt worthy of his fans' adoration. *I'm something special — more special than you are*, he seemed to be saying. He told his fans that because he was exhausted from playing this "gig," he'd be signing autographs for only a short time. His ego was so obviously great that he succeeded in turning off many of the fans who'd gone to much trouble and expense to come see him. I heard one disappointed admirer say with a shrug as he walked away, "Sounds like he's his own biggest fan."

The other band was signing autographs at the other end of the stage. What a contrast! Rather than building their own egos, they were using their influence as Christian celebrities to minister to the needs of the young people who had come to them. I watched one of the group members sit for fifteen minutes talking with a paraplegic teen who had been wheeled up to get an autograph. Another band member sat cross-legged on the floor, listening to the spiritual struggles of a searching young man.

Those giving, self-sacrificing Christian performers reminded me of diamonds. Why are diamonds among the most beautiful and valuable gems in the world? Because of their brilliance. You can see all the colors of the rainbow in a diamond's sparkle! Why is a diamond so brilliant? Because it reflects and passes on all the light that comes its way.

Think, on the other hand, of a lump of black coal. It has almost the same chemical makeup as the diamond, but how often have you seen a group of people standing around ooh-ing and ah-ing over a lump of coal, or a young woman proudly holding up her engagement ring featuring a hunk of coal? The difference is that black *absorbs* light. Soaks it in. Keeps it rather than passes it on to share with others.

It's easy to absorb attention and praise in the mistaken belief that it makes us brilliant. That egotistical young musician made that mistake—and he looked anything but brilliant to his disappointed young fans. The other Christian band knew the truth—that we are lifted from the pettiness of egotism when we reflect back adoration and praise to Jesus Christ while at the same time reflecting his love to those around us. Then we shine like diamonds!

Most of us aren't famous musical performers. Still, we each have opportunities to build our own egos at the expense of others, or instead to build up others around us and glorify Christ at the same time.

To soak the light in, or to reflect it. The choice is ours.

Don't be a lump of coal. Be a diamond!

VERSE OF THE DAY:

Do not think of yourself more highly than you ought, but rather think of yourself with sober judgment, in accordance with the measure of faith God has given you.
—Romans 12:3

HEY!

Want to read what Jesus said about pride? It's in Luke 14:7-11. And here are a couple of great proverbs about big egos: Proverbs 26:12 and 27:2.

JUST DO IT:

Our egos are usually more sensitive in some areas than in others. For instance, somebody who may not care whether people think of him as a great student or a great athlete may be very vain about his appearance. Or someone who doesn't take great pains about her appearance may be angry if she isn't considered the best singer in the school chorus.

What are *your* areas of "ego alert"? What are you more sensitive and vain about than other things? Make a list of those areas. Knowing what they are will help you watch for the times you're trying to gather praise to yourself at the expense of others and glorifying yourself rather than Christ.

When you look for opportunities to meet the needs of others and reflect the love of Christ, you shine like a diamond. Watch for such an opportunity today.

At our house we have a computer program that can guess the name of any animal you can think of. It asks a series of questions that narrow the possibilities of size, habitat, and other variables until finally it announces the name of the animal—even though the person playing the game has never verbalized it.

WHO'S SMARTER— YOU OR THE COMPUTER?

How did a computer program get so smart? It learned from its mistakes. When we first got the program, it could guess only a few animals. But every time it guessed wrong, the computer would ask the user a question. Once, for instance, it guessed "frog" when I was thinking "alligator."

"How was I wrong?" the computer asked. "In what way does a frog differ from an alligator?"

I typed an answer, and the program retained that information so that it would never make the same mistake again. Like the robot in the movie *Short Circuit*, the computer sought input; it requested as much information as possible in order to be as correct as possible in the future.

It's as if that computer had heard something that was once said by T. J. Watson, founder of IBM: *Success is on the far side of failure.*

And that's good news, because everybody—child, teenager, and grown-up—makes mistakes. (Even *I* made a mistake once.) And some of those mistakes are lulus. We fail, big time. But don't be discouraged. Those failures, those mistakes, can be the stepping-stones to success.

Okay, I admit that's not easy to believe when you've just failed a history test and you have to tell your parents. It's doubtful that your parents will see this as an opportunity for growth. More likely, they'll see it as an opportunity to ground you for a million years. (Which you, in turn, could choose to see as an opportunity to get to know the inside of your house—intimately!) But after that million years is over, you might even find that you've learned something—such as new attitudes toward school, or new study habits. And because of what you've learned, next time you'll do better.

Just like that computer.

The computer, of course, has one major advantage over you. At no time, when it failed to correctly identify the animal I had chosen, did I put it on restriction for a million years. (Besides, computers don't party much anyway!)

VERSE OF THE DAY:

Instruct a wise man and he will be wiser still;
teach a righteous man and he will add to his learning. —*Proverbs 9:9*

HEY!

Jesus once met a woman who had really *sinned. Want to know what he said to her? Read John 8:1-11.*

JUST DO IT:

In that passage in John 8, Jesus wanted the woman to learn from her sin so that she would not commit that sin anymore. Sometime today, make a list of about a half-dozen mistakes you've made over the past week. They can be either intentional sins, like lying to your parents and getting put on restriction—or little mistakes, such as wearing an outfit to school that didn't go together and getting teased about it. When you've got your list, confess the intentional sins and ask for wisdom to learn from your mistakes. Then, next to each item on your list, write what you learned from the experience and what you'll do differently next time.

Look at it this way: If the experiences were a pain to begin with, then they might as well count for something. Why let all that pain go to waste?

IT'S A SMALL WORLD AFTER ALL?

The world's a lot smaller place than it used to be. And I'm not talking about the fact that you can jet anywhere you want in a very short time, or that you can telephone anywhere in less. I'm talking about the fact that two thousand years ago, when Christ was here, there were only three hundred million people alive on Earth — now there are 4.5 billion.

That's a lot of people. And it means that each of us gets a much smaller piece of the planet than people got two thousand years ago.

But wait. It gets smaller still. Or at least it looked much smaller to the Apollo astronauts when they traveled 238,857 miles to the moon (that's about thirty times Earth's diameter). When they looked back at Earth, it looked like a little marble.

Of course, they were really pretty close to Earth. A lot closer than the sun, which is 93 million miles away. Better take a sack lunch.

And no wonder Earth didn't look very big: Jupiter, the sun's largest planet, is more than eleven times as big across as Earth. The sun is 109 times as big across as Earth. And some stars are one thousand times as big across as the sun.

The closest star is just over four light-years away — about twenty trillion miles. The galaxy we're part of — the Milky Way — is shaped like a flattened disk about one hundred thousand light-years in diameter. The sun is definitely important to us, but it's only one of millions upon millions of stars in the Milky Way.

And there are other galaxies in space. About ten billion of them at last count — give or take a billion. Some of them are more than a billion light-years away. (I could give you that distance in miles, but my page isn't big enough.)

Small world.

Makes you wish Protagoras were alive today, doesn't it? You say, "Who's Protagoras?"

Protagoras was the Greek philosopher who said, a couple of thousand years ago: "Man is the measure of all things."

Wouldn't it be interesting to show him that he's only one of 4.5 billion people on a planet ninety-three million miles from the nearest star, which is only one of more than a billion stars in this galaxy, which is only one of ten billion galaxies? (We'd better break it to him gently that these estimates are good only until scientists develop more powerful telescopes.)

Suddenly the whole planetful of humans seems about as important as the dust specks I wiped off my glasses this morning.

Except for one thing.

You see, when God finished creating all of those stars and galaxies and planets and comets, he decided to make a special kind of being—one who would be in his own image. So he took some dust from that one teensy dust-speck planet, Earth, and he formed that special being, and he called it Man.

And he said, "That's good." And he loved Man. He loved Man so much that he gave up the single most precious thing in the universe—his own Son—to restore the companionship that Man had selfishly destroyed.

And he still loves us. Not just as a bunch of people but each of us separately—you and me. By name. Suddenly the universe seems like a much friendlier place. And a little smaller.

VERSE OF THE DAY:

When I consider your heavens,
the work of your fingers,
the moon and the stars,
which you have set in place,
what is man that you are mindful of him,
the son of man that you care for him?
You made him a little lower than the heavenly beings
and crowned him with glory and honor.   —Psalm 8:3-5

HEY!

You may be a tiny speck in the universe, but you have no reason to fear. Read about it in Matthew 10:29-31.

THINK ABOUT IT:

Spend some time today just trying to imagine the immensity and power of God. He created us individually, with all of our quirks and talents, at the same time he was keeping the universe spinning with the other hand!

Some awesome God!

And now contemplate this incredible fact: We're more than just a favorite part of his creation. We're his adopted sons and daughters. He loves us as his own children.

THE PIT AND THE PENDULUM

In my speech class in college I was assigned to prepare a lesson to teach my class—any lesson, as long as it was taught creatively. I taught the law of the pendulum.

Here's how that law is stated: A pendulum can never return to a point higher than the point from which it is released. Because of friction and gravity, it will form a smaller and smaller arc each time it swings, until finally it stops. Unless, of course, somebody gives it a push.

I spent the first twenty minutes of my presentation explaining this principle to the class. I even demonstrated the law with a toy top hanging from a string pinned to the blackboard. I made a mark on the blackboard, where I let the top go, and then I marked the spot it reached on each successively shorter swing. It took less than a minute for the top to complete its swinging and come to rest. When I finished the demonstration, the markings on the blackboard proved my point.

"How many of you believe that the law of the pendulum is true?" I asked the class. All hands flew up, including the teacher's. As the class applauded my presentation, he moved toward the front, thinking that I was through. But I had only just begun.

Hanging from the steel ceiling beams in the middle of the room was a large pendulum I had made from 250 pounds of weight-lifting discs and parachute cord. This was a *big* pendulum. I invited the teacher to climb up on a table and sit in a chair with the back of his head against a cement wall. Then I brought the 250 pounds of metal up to his nose. "If the law of the pendulum is true," I said, "then when I release this mass of metal, it will swing across the room and return short of where I am holding it right now. Your nose will be in no danger. Now—do you believe that the law of the pendulum is true?" I asked, looking him right in the eye.

There was a long pause. Huge beads of sweat formed on his upper lip, and one drop hung precariously from the very end of his nose. Then, weakly, he nodded and whispered, "Yes." I released the pendulum.

It made a swishing sound as it arced across the room. At the far end of its swing, it paused momentarily and started back. I have never seen a man move so fast in my life! He literally dived from the table.

Carefully, I stepped around the still-swinging pendulum and asked the class, "Does he believe in the law of the pendulum?" In unison they answered, "No!"

My professor *understood* the law but was unwilling to trust his nose to it. After a short discussion, a student volunteered to sit in the chair. Even though his face contorted in fear as the pendulum started back, he stayed put. It stopped an inch from his nose and swung away from him again. Now his faith in that law was strengthened. The next time the pendulum swung, he didn't even blink.

When you go beyond just knowing about God and begin to trust him with your life, that's when you really know what you believe. As you study the Bible and discover the principles God has put for you there, put them into practice in your life. It's risky business. It's not always easy to obey God in this way, but when you trust your nose to what you say you believe—and discover that he is faithful—your faith will be strengthened.

And there's no better time to do that than right now.

VERSE OF THE DAY:

Do not merely listen to the word, and so deceive yourselves. Do what it says. Anyone who listens to the word but does not do what it says is like a man who looks at his face in a mirror and, after looking at himself, goes away and immediately forgets what he looks like. But the man who looks intently into the perfect law that gives freedom and continues to do this —not forgetting what he has heard but doing it —he will be blessed in what he does. —James 1:22-26

HEY!

James has even more to say about obeying the Bible than what he says in those verses. Read more in James 2:14-24.

JUST DO IT:

Have you ever read something in the Bible that you really felt you needed to put into practice in your life, but instead you just blew it off? Silly question—we've *all* done that. But that doesn't mean it's a good idea. Maybe now would be a good time to jot down some of those actions you feel you needed to take or changes you feel you needed to make, and act on them. It's not too late. God's law is as dependable as the law of the pendulum.

You can trust your nose to it.

Cipher in the Snow is one of the most powerful films I have ever seen. It's based on the true story of a young boy who stepped off the school bus one day and collapsed, dead in the snow. During the investigation of his death, they discovered that no one could remember him. In the minds of everyone who knew him, he was a cipher, a zero. Some of his teachers couldn't even remember his having been in their classes; at home, he was ignored and treated as though he had no worth.

So why did he die? Doctors found no apparent cause of death. The most likely explanation, observers concluded, was that he finally came to believe that he was zero. A zero has no reason for being, so the boy simply died quietly in a snowbank. He truly became zero.

"What a morbid story!" you may be saying. "Why depress us by talking about something we can't do anything about anyway, even if we want to? We didn't know the guy, and besides, it's too late—he's dead."

Not really. He's still around. He's walking the halls of your school. He sits by you in algebra.

She eats lunch all by herself over near the door so she can make a quick getaway. You walk past her every day, and you haven't noticed her yet.

He goes to your church but always leaves right after the service so he won't have to stand around by himself with nobody to talk to.

She's the one who got up the nerve to say "hi" to you in gym class one day, but your friends were calling you and, not really aware that you were hurting her feelings, you left her standing there.

Maybe you're saying, "Hey, not me! I try to be nice to the people around me. I try not to hurt people's feelings. It's not my fault if my school's full of people I don't know. I can't be responsible for *everybody!*"

True. But you can be responsible for somebody.

And no matter how many excuses I come up with and how little time I have, I still can't escape that little voice in my head that says, "I was hungry and you gave me nothing to eat, I was thirsty and you gave me nothing to drink, I was a stranger and you did not invite me in, I needed clothes and you did not clothe me" (Matt. 25:42, 43).

Those ciphers, those nobodies, all around us represent Jesus. And each of us has to decide for himself or herself how to respond to the Jesus who sits beside us in algebra—afraid, alone, and crying inside.

VERSE OF THE DAY:

Whatever you did for one of the least of these brothers of mine, you did for me.
—*Matthew. 25:40*

HEY!

Read the whole story in Matthew 25:31-46.

JUST DO IT:

Did you read Matthew 25:31-46? Are you a sheep or a goat most of the time? Can you think right now of some "ciphers" in your school, church, or neighborhood whose lives you can make a difference in? Write down (you'll remember it better if you write it down) the ways you're going to do that. Open your eyes to those around you who need your smile, or a kind word. Then, when you see those people next, remember who they are: "Whatever you did for one of the least of these brothers of mine ..."

E ver watch a bunch of sheep out running in the field? They're weird! There can be a hundred of them out there, all running the same direction, and one of them—probably some rebellious sheep with a Mohawk, dressed in black leather, and an earring in his nose—will think: *I'm gonna go a different way.* So he turns. You know what the rest of them do? They turn, too! They don't even think about it. One turns, they all turn.

FOLLOW THE LEADER

I hate to say it, but we're a lot like sheep. Not that we like to go running across the fields with an earring through our nose, but that we're a lot better at following somebody else than we are at choosing our own direction.

When we're around our friends, isn't it true that much of the time we don't *want* to be any different from them in any way? However they dress, however they talk, whatever they do—that's how we dress and talk and act, too. Right?

But what's even scarier is that we want to *believe* just what they believe. I know few people who could answer quickly if you ask them what they believe, what they live for. And I know even fewer who have the courage to pay the price to *live* what they believe. Most people I know simply follow somebody else—whoever they're around. When they're at church, they act the way church people want them to act. When they're at home, they act the way their family wants them to act. When they're with friends, they act the way their friends want them to act.

Like chameleons, those little lizards that can change their color to match whatever background they happen to be near so they don't stand out.

That isn't what God wants for us. Oh, he knows we're like sheep, all right. He's the one who *told* us we are like sheep. But the only one he wants us to follow is the Good Shepherd, Jesus Christ. Around anybody else, we need to remember that sometimes we have to put our foot down and say, "Not this sheep."

VERSE OF THE DAY:

Be on your guard; stand firm in the faith; be men of courage, be strong.
—1 Corinthians 16:13

HEY!

Want to read about somebody who refused to follow the crowd? Read Daniel 6.

JUST DO IT:

Today's verse starts, "Be on your guard." Practice that today. Compromising situations have a way of slipping up on us. Maybe something we really don't think God would want us to say slips out just because we're standing around with a bunch of others who are talking that way. Maybe we find ourselves insulting somebody just because everybody else is doing it. Today, keep your eyes and ears open to what's going on around you. Are there temptations to disobey God by just going along with the crowd? "Be on your guard."

I met Diane in college. We were both working our way through school; we peeled potatoes together.

"IS THIS ALL I GET?"

But I didn't realize at first how beautiful she was, because she wore a pair of glasses that concealed her beauty. You've seen pictures of those butterfly glasses? The ones with wings?

One day she leaned over that vat of potatoes, and the glasses fell off. Splat! My first thought was, *Yuck! I'm not eating those potatoes!* Then she looked up, confused, and I got a good look at her face without the glasses for the very first time. She was beautiful! I decided I'd eat the glasses if I had to.

But, being a gentleman, I fished the glasses out of the vat of potatoes and made up my mind that one day I'd give that girl a gift that complemented her beauty in a way those glasses never could. Months later, I walked into a jewelry store to buy that gift—a diamond. I found the diamond I wanted, laid it on the counter, and told the jeweler about the beautiful girl I was going to marry. "Charge it!" I said proudly.

He said, "Do you have any credit?"

I said, "Uh—I don't *think* so, but I'd be glad to get some. How do I get some?"

He said, "You get credit by charging something."

I said, "Great! Charge it."

He said, "I can't let you charge it unless you have credit."

I looked at him for a moment, then said, "You mean I can't get credit until I have credit, and I can't have credit until I get credit?"

He just smiled.

So I went back home and I sold everything I owned—even my most prized possession, my hunting bow and arrows. Finally I had a big enough down payment on the ring to influence the jeweler to let me charge the rest.

I brought Diane to my parents' house after a date. We sat down on the couch, the diamond ring in my pocket, and I put my arm around her and told her that I loved her very much. Then I took her ring off her finger and told her, "Someday I'm going to replace this with a diamond."

27

Understand that I had been preparing Diane for this moment for weeks. Dozens of times I had taken that ring of hers off her finger and said, "Someday I'm going to replace this with a diamond." She was used to hearing it. She was also used to finding her old ring back on her finger, not a new diamond.

But this time, the diamond ring went onto her finger, and her old ring went into my pocket.

And, naturally, she didn't bother to look. This had happened too many times before. Twenty minutes went by. She went into the kitchen to get us a Coke, and suddenly from the kitchen came an incredible scream. She ran back into the room, threw her arms around me, knocked me over, and we broke a coffee table. It was great!

I was as delighted as she was. I was giving her what I considered to be an incredible gift—not just a ring but the rest of my life—and she received it with joy and gladness and enthusiasm.

But just imagine how I'd have felt if Diane had come out of the kitchen and said, "Is this as good as you could do? Couldn't you afford a bigger diamond?"

I don't know what I'd have done. But I know there'd have been no joy in my heart that night.

We have the same opportunity that Diane had that night. When we get up each day, we can thank God for the incredible gift of life. We can thank Jesus that he died on the cross for us so that we can have a relationship with God now and eternal life, too. That's a gift worth more than a million diamonds.

Or we can say, "Is this it? Couldn't you have worked it so I could enjoy the pleasures of sin a little more? Why is being a Christian such a drag? Couldn't you have made me better looking? Or more talented? Or rich? And why is it raining today? Is this all I get?"

God will be there today to meet your every need. He will provide the strength you need in difficult times. How will you respond?

VERSE OF THE DAY:

But I will sing of your strength,
in the morning I will sing of your love;
for you are my fortress,
my refuge in times of trouble.

—Psalms 59:16

HEY!

Want to read about a teenager who recognized God's power and accepted the help he offered? Read the story of David and Goliath in 1 Samuel 17.

JUST DO IT:

Take that last line of today's reading as a serious question: How *will* you respond to God's offer to help you today? Write down two or three specific things you'll do today for which you'll need to depend on God or allow him to give you the help you need. At the end of the day, review your list to see how well you did.

God offers us a wonderful gift—even better than a diamond engagement ring! Let's accept it with gratitude.

WHAT! ME WORRY?

I read a lot, and every now and then I'll come across something that blasts into my mind with such power that it stays with me for years. That's how I felt when I read the following poem by Elizabeth Cheney, "Overheard in an Orchard":

> Said the Robin to the Sparrow:
> "I should really like to know
> Why these anxious human beings
> Rush about and worry so."

> Said the Sparrow to the Robin:
> "Friend, I think that it must be
> That they have no heavenly Father
> Such as cares for you and me."

When I read that, my first thought was, *Wow—what a profound truth! Even the little birds out in the orchard have more faith than we do. They know God's going to take care of them.*

And then came my second thought: *Hey, wait a minute. It's easy for birds and animals to trust God. Their needs are very simple. Ours are very complex. We need clothes, medical care, love, and affirmation, family stability, help getting through school—plenty of things that robins and sparrows almost never think about. And we're also smart enough to know how many things can go wrong in our getting those things. I mean, even robins and sparrows would worry if they could read the weather report!*

Those things are true. But I still like the poem because it reminds me of this truth: God *has* promised to meet our needs in the same way he meets the needs of the robin and the sparrow. "And my God will meet all your needs according to his glorious riches in Christ Jesus," the Bible says in Philippians 4:19. We can believe that he will—and relax. Or we can refuse to believe it—and worry. It's up to us.

I know. I'm making it sound easier than it is. We often feel that we have needs that are unmet. If God is supposed to be meeting those needs, then where is he?

It's also true that we sometimes mix up our needs with our desires. God didn't say that he was going to give us whatever we want—he said he was going to give us whatever we *need*. And he knows our needs better than we do.

We also have a tendency to want things right *now*. God sometimes makes us wait.

There's a great definition of faith in Hebrews 11:1: "Now faith is being sure of what we hope for and certain of what we do not see." It's going to take faith—being sure of what we hope for and certain of what we do not see—to believe that God is going to meet our needs in the same way he meets the robin's and the sparrow's.

But it sure beats running around wringing our hands and moaning about all the things we're afraid will happen.

I choose to trust God.

If some stupid bird can do it, so can I.

VERSE OF THE DAY:

Cast all your anxiety upon him because he cares for you. —1 Peter 5:7

HEY!

The all-time greatest comment on worry came from Jesus himself in the Sermon on the Mount. It's not long. Read it in Matthew 6:25-34.

JUST DO IT:

Are you a worrier? That's a hard habit to break. You can start by reading and trying to believe the verses given above, but you also need an action plan. How are you going to break the bad habit of worry? What are you going to do the next time you feel anxiety about the future creeping up on you? Write down the steps you'll take. Then use them!

WATCH WHERE YOU RUN

A few years ago I moved into a new house, with a lake nearby. *Great,* I thought, *what a wonderful place to run in the mornings.* And I started having my morning workouts running around that lake every day.

And it *was* a great place—for several months. Then one morning I was enjoying the fresh air, maybe praying a little as I ran, daydreaming—and somebody was hiding back in the bushes with a two-by-four in his hand, saying, "I'm gonna get that guy."

A half hour later I stumbled back home, bruised and sore, beaten half-senseless. But the hard part wasn't the injuries, the hard part wasn't the pain. The hard part was asking myself: *Why? What did I do that I deserved this?*

Why is it that we tend to feel guilty when things go bad whether we were really to blame or not? Maybe one of the reasons is that we don't readily accept God's forgiveness. We've *all* sinned. Many times. The Bible says in Romans 3:23, "All have sinned and fall short of the glory of God," and in Romans 6:23, "The wages of sin is death." We know we've sinned, we know we deserve punishment, and sometimes we just accept whatever punishment comes our way as being nothing more than we deserve.

But that isn't true. Because there are a few things left out of that explanation. One is that Christ died to pay for those sins. Another is that because Christ paid the penalty for those sins, God is able not only to forgive us but to remove the sin completely.

So when that guy with the two-by-four jumped me, *it had nothing to do with me at all!* He was just a weirdo with a two-by-four; he wasn't some avenging angel sent by God to pay me back for the bird I ran over with my bike as a kid. Jesus already paid for my sins. So when I ask myself, *Why is God doing this to me,* the answer is that he *isn't* doing this to me. God is not paying me back. My attacker chose any victim who happened by and didn't look dangerous. (If you ever see me in a pair of running shorts, you'll know why I didn't look dangerous. Gross, maybe, but not dangerous. More like the Pillsbury Dough

Boy.) He could just as easily have chosen somebody else, but by chance he chose me.

But that guy was a stranger. What about when a *friend* turns against you, and you can't think of anything you've done to deserve it? What if a parent drinks too much and knocks you around? Girls, what if some guy forces himself on you while you're out on a date? When the pain is coming from someone we know and like, then it's even easier to blame ourselves. *My dad hit me because I've been bad; I deserved it. My boyfriend ripped my blouse open because I teased him, or because I came on too strong; it was my fault.*

No. A thousand times no. Christ paid the penalty for our sin; when someone treats us with disrespect or hostility or violence, we don't have to accept it as our fault.

Let's make sure we understand the message of the Cross. It means that the debt is *paid*. Our sins are forgiven, and in God's eyes forgiven means *gone*. We may have hurt others by our sins, and we'll need to ask their forgiveness, too—but God isn't about to send a guy with a two-by-four (or an abusive parent, or a disrespectful boyfriend) to take it out of our hides.

When Jesus Christ does something, he does it completely. Your pain won't add anything to the job he's already finished.

VERSE OF THE DAY:

Therefore, there is now no condemnation for those who are in Christ Jesus, because through Christ Jesus the law of the Spirit of Life set me free from the law of sin and death.   —Romans 8:1, 2

HEY!

If you really don't feel forgiven yet, read 1 John 1:9 and put it to use. Is there any sin so great God that can't forgive it? Read Romans 8:31-39.

JUST DO IT:

Can you think of any ways in which you're making yourself "pay" for your sins by allowing an abusive situation to continue or by blaming yourself for bad things that have happened? If so, you deserve better. Write down the steps you're going to take to change that situation. Is there a friend or teacher or pastor whose help you need in changing this situation? Don't hesitate to get help if you feel the need for it.

And most of all, remember that God sent Jesus to die to take your guilt away. Don't hang onto it.

Good luck! Remember Romans 8:31: "If God is for us, who can be against us?"

I sn't this a great story?

BUTTING HEADS

Two battleships assigned to the training squadron had been on maneuvers in heavy weather for several days. I was serving on the lead battleship and was on the watch on the bridge as night fell. The visibility was poor with patchy fog, so the captain remained on the bridge, keeping an eye on all activities.

Shortly after dark, the lookout on the wing of the bridge reported, "Light, bearing on the starboard bow."

"Is it steady or moving astern?" the captain called out.

Lookout replied, "Steady, captain," which meant we were on a dangerous collision course with that ship.

The captain then called to the signalman, "Signal that ship: We are on a collision course, advise you change course 20 degrees."

Back came a signal, "Advisable for you to change course 20 degrees."

The captain said: "Send: I'm a captain, change course 20 degrees."

"I'm a seaman second class," came the reply. "You had better change course 20 degrees."

By that time, the captain was furious. He spat out: "Send, I'm a battleship. Change course 20 degrees."

Back came the flashing light, "I'm a lighthouse."

We changed course.[1]

Funny story. But also true of many of the conversations we have with our friends, our parents, our brothers and sisters. We're so busy trying to make our point that we don't listen to what the other is saying.

Once I watched two cars in a parking lot run head-on into each other. Now, maybe they weren't watching where they were going; maybe they were looking for parking places, or changing the radio station or something. Or maybe they saw the other car coming and were just too stubborn to be the first one to turn. I can imagine what was going through their minds as they approached each other:

Who does he think he is, cruising along like this, just expecting that I'll turn first? Does he think he owns the parking lot? Let him be the one to turn first! He's just trying to take my parking spot, that's all, and I'm not going to let him get away with it! Move it, buddy! If you think you're going to push me around, you're

—CRASH!

At least the captain of the battleship knew when he was beat.

Somehow, I don't think that the pattern God wants us to follow in our relationships with our friends and family members is the pattern of butting heads until one person's head gets too sore and he gives up. I think he'd prefer the pattern of mutual respect, give-and-take, trying to understand the thoughts and ideas of the other. I think God would prefer that we seek first to understand and then to be understood.

Even the Golden Rule should tell us that much.

More easily said than done, right? Especially with family members. But most of our arguments happen because both parties are too stubborn to listen and too angry to stop talking.

So here's a plan. You want to *really* freak your brothers or sisters out? Next time they try to start an argument, actually *listen* to them! Then ask them questions about what they're saying, to find out more about how they feel. The look on their faces will be worth more than winning any argument.

VERSE OF THE DAY:
Everyone should be quick to listen, slow to speak, and slow to become angry.
—James 1:19

HEY!
Ephesians 4:29-32 gives some great principles for Christians to follow in conversation and relationships—tough but great!

JUST DO IT:

Christianity starts at home. And nobody knows better than you just how tough it can be to be a Christian at home. But let's start to put today's verse to work at home first, before anywhere else. "Quick to listen, slow to speak, slow to become angry." Wow! How on earth are you going to do that? God will help, of course, if you ask him, but you've got to come up with a plan. Begin thinking of that plan now, and as you come up with ideas, write them down. As you go through the day, keep a record of the times you have a chance to apply those ideas.

Good luck!

[1]Stephen R. Covey, *The Seven Habits of Highly Effective People* (New York: Simon and Schuster, 1989), 33.

A REAL MAN

Have you ever seen those pictures of Jesus that make him look like some weak, pushover sissy who's afraid to get his hands dirty? I hate those pictures! It isn't just that I don't want to think of Jesus that way— it's that the Bible doesn't describe him that way.

I mean, think about it. Jesus chose his followers from among some of the toughest, roughest men on the planet. They were strong, physical, and dirty; they were probably hard drinkers and foul-mouthed. (Have you ever heard the term, "cuss like a sailor"?) These guys had the reputation of today's longshoremen.

Jesus didn't even negotiate with them. He didn't go down to the shore and call to them as they got off their boats, "Gentlemen! Let's sit down and talk a minute. I've got something to offer that I think will interest you. Once you understand the benefits of following me ..."

Nothing like that. He walked up to them and said, "Follow me."

And they *did!* These rough-and-tumble, not-afraid-of-anything fishermen—two of them had the nickname "The Sons of Thunder" (bet the local police department loved them!)—dropped their nets on the spot and walked off with Jesus.

You can bet they wouldn't have dropped their nets and followed your run-of-the-mill Twinkie. Jesus was enough of a man to command not only the respect but the obedience of some of the toughest men on earth.

And other incidents in his life demonstrated why.

One day he walked into the temple courtyard and found the money changers and sacrifice-sellers with their tables set up, cheating the worshippers and making a fortune doing it—right in God's house! You've heard the story. Jesus didn't turn to his men and say, "Get those crooks out of here." He walked up to those tables and dumped them over. Can't you just see it? Coins rolling all over, doves flying all around, lambs bleating, people shouting, tables crashing—and then he grabbed a whip and chased all those cheats out of the courtyard! And he didn't mince words. "You've changed my Father's house into a den of thieves!" he yelled.

I love that story. And I love the stories about his casting out demons just by telling them who he was. "I'm Jesus—and you're history."

Why is this important? Because if we're Christians, if we bear his name, we need to know whom we're following. He was not some weakling. He was the most powerful human being ever to walk the earth. And not just because he ordered fishermen around and chased thieves out of the temple—but because he changed the course of history and changed forever the way in which we relate to God. And because he was the only person to be not only human but also God.

So ignore those Twinkie pictures.

Instead, learn what the Bible says about Jesus, the real man—and living God.

VERSE OF THE DAY:

And Jesus grew in wisdom and stature, and in favor with God and men.

—Luke 2:52

HEY!

The story of Jesus' calling the fishermen is found in Luke 5:1-11. In John 2:13-16 you can read about Jesus' driving the merchants out of the temple.

JUST DO IT:

After you've read the passages of Scripture listed above, try this experiment: Today, whenever something comes up that requires you to take a stand, ask yourself, "How would the Jesus who threw the moneychangers out of the temple handle this situation?" Would he sit back and say nothing? Would he run away? Would he step in and take care of it himself? The same God who called the fishermen, cast out demons, and threw out the money changers is your God.

PRAYING ON THE RUN

Every morning I run around the lake, and as I run, I talk to God. Some mornings I say, "God, thank you for the wonderful morning! Thanks for the trees, and the leaves, and everything else you made. It's just so great to be alive!" Other mornings I pray, "God, I feel terrible. Where are you, anyway? I don't feel you near me. My life's a mess, and I don't know what to do!"

And I pray all this out loud—which keeps other people from jogging near me!

A woman once asked me, very critically, "Don't you kneel when you pray?" No—I tried it once, but I only made it about halfway round the lake. It hurt so bad!

But the question isn't really whether we kneel when we pray, or whether it's okay to pray out loud in public and freak people out. The question is: How honest are we with God when we pray? When I'm angry with God, or when I'm feeling lousy, I let him know it. "God, I don't think it's fair! God, I feel like you let me down. God, I feel absolutely miserable."

I've heard people say, "That's sacrilegious. You shouldn't talk to God that way." But how do you *think* God wants us to talk to him? Do you think he wants us to lie? Isn't that what we're doing when we say, "God, I'm feeling good today; glad to be here," when really we're angry or afraid or discouraged? We're afraid to tell him the truth. We're afraid that it's a sin to feel that way.

David never worried about that when he prayed. In the Psalms he was about as honest with God as he could be. He said things like, "I am feeble and utterly crushed; I groan in anguish of heart" (Psalm 38:8) and "My God, my God, why have you forsaken me? Why are you so far from saving me...? I cry out by day, but you do not answer" (Psalm 22:1, 2).

Let's be honest with God. He *knows* how we're feeling anyway. So level with him. He's better able to help us with our feelings of anger or unbelief when we tell him the truth.

VERSE OF THE DAY:

Let us then approach the throne of grace with confidence, so that we may receive mercy and find grace to help us in our time of need. —*Hebrews 4:16*

HEY!

Do you really think God will respond to your prayers? Read Luke 18:1-7 —and don't give up!

JUST DO IT:

For the next week, try something a little different in your prayers. Be completely honest with God about how you're feeling. Feeling angry toward God because something terrible has happened? Tell him that. Feeling unworthy, unloved, humiliated, forsaken, lonely? Feel like nothing will ever be right again? Tell him that, too. And in spite of all that, praise him because he is God. Ask him to help you with your feelings, thank him for listening, and say amen. God will hear you.

He *won't* strike you with lightning for your honesty. But he *will* surround you with love.

"GUESS WHAT—I'M GOING TO DIE!"

Imagine sitting down one day with your best friend—the person who's closest to you in the whole world, and that person says to you, "I have something very important to say: I'm going to die soon!"

Tell me *that* wouldn't freak you out! But imagine that your friend then says, "Hey—the reason I'm telling you this is so you won't worry about it. I want you to relax and be at peace."

No way! A death announcement is not exactly your most effective tranquilizer.

Sounds strange—but that's exactly what Jesus told his disciples in John 16. After telling them that he was going to die, he told them that they shouldn't get all upset about it. And he had another piece of great information for them: For the rest of their lives, they would have hassles, temptations, and trials!

What! Read the passage and see for yourself: John 13:33-38 and 15:18-16:3. Can't you just imagine the disciples sitting there saying, "Oh, great, Lord—now what's the *bad* news?"

But I'll tell you the truth: That's a great message because it frees us from a mistaken notion that many of us have. We think that if we're good, things will go well—that God will make sure nothing goes wrong. And if we're bad, God will make bad things happen. And that, my friend, is a dangerous misconception—because if we believe that, we think that all the bad things that happen in our lives are our own fault!

Some of the bad things that happen to us, of course, are the direct result of our bad choices. If you don't study, you'll fail. If you disobey your parents, you'll probably end up grounded. But even if you play by the rules, bad stuff still happens—and it isn't your fault.

When I talk to kids whose parents have split up, I find that most of them blame themselves. I even find that when I talk to kids who've had a death in the family, I have to reassure them that it wasn't their fault! They think of God as a cosmic policeman sitting up there waiting for them to mess up and when they do, he's gonna get 'em!

But that's just not true. And that's what's so cool about what Jesus told the disciples that day. He told them ahead of time that they would have problems all their lives—but *not* because of anything they did or didn't do! It's a part of being alive. *Their* job is just to do the best they can when all the bad stuff comes down.

I don't know about you, but I'm glad Jesus gave us that message. It frees me from having to feel guilty every time something goes wrong. As the saying goes, the rain falls on the just and the unjust alike. And when bad things happen, it isn't because God is punishing you. It's because you're alive.

Jesus doesn't want us burdened with guilt. Instead, we can find joy even in the midst of problems—because Jesus has already won the battle, and he wants to share the victory with us.

VERSE OF THE DAY:

"I have told you these things, so that in me you may have peace. In this world you will have trouble. But take heart! I have overcome the world." —John 16:33

HEY!

Do you think that God can work for your good even through the mistakes you make? Read Romans 8:28.

JUST DO IT:

What sins or mistakes you've made are plaguing you with worry right now? Figure out what's bothering you the most, and then ask yourself: *Is this the result of something I did that I need to ask forgiveness for?* If the answer's yes, talk to the people you've hurt, admit what you did wrong, and ask their forgiveness. But if the thing you're worried about is just a mistake, then learn from it and move on. You don't need to feel guilty over everything! Jesus went to the cross to spare us from that.

"HOW CAN YOU GIVE YOUR OWN SELF A SHOT?"

DAVE

As part of my treatment for leukemia, I had to inject myself with Interferon three times a week for a year. My daughter Beth, in first grade then, watched between her fingers one day as I injected my leg, and she asked, "How can you give your own self a shot? Doesn't it hurt?"

"It doesn't hurt much if I think about being well some day," I replied.

Like the football coach who motivates himself to endure the long months of hard work by putting a picture of the championship trophy in front of his desk, or the salesman who looks every night at the picture of his dream sailboat to make the long hours of sales calls worthwhile, I thought about the end result and ignored the periods of discomfort. When the leukemia was under control and I was feeling healthy again, the pain I'd gone through to get there seemed insignificant.

Whether we like to hear it or not, following Christ has some costs. Maybe you've already encountered some of those costs, and maybe not. But you will. Friends who don't like the new you and decide they don't want you to be part of their group anymore. Things you really want to do that now, because you're a Christian and have a different set of values, you choose—reluctantly—not to do. Teasing and hostility from people who, for one reason or another, don't like Christians. A romantic relationship you have to break off because your girlfriend or boyfriend doesn't share your beliefs and wants to take that relationship in directions you don't feel you can go. All of those—and many more—are some of the costs you pay for being a Christian.

But like the shots I had to give myself for my leukemia, those costs pay off in the end. Anything worth doing, in fact, has costs. When your school's football team wins the championship, those sitting in the stands and cheering haven't paid the costs. But the players sweating on the field surely have, in countless hours of practicing, drilling, working, and concentrating—time that they'd rather have spent doing something else, but they knew that hard work and practice are the cost of success.

When you see two people whose marriage is working well, who love each other and help each other, then you're looking at two people who've worked hard on their marriage. Marriage isn't easy, and making it work involves hours of making mistakes and then working through them, hours of talking, hours of thinking and giving and sharing, sometimes hours of arguing and hours in a marriage counselor's office. But the end result is worth the pain and effort.

Christ offers us the same hope to help us deal with the costs of being a Christian: Endure the unpleasantness because in the end the reward will be well worth it.

VERSE OF THE DAY:

"Blessed are you when people insult you, persecute you and falsely say all kinds of evil against you because of me. Rejoice and be glad, because great is your reward in heaven."   *—Luke 9:23*

HEY!

Want to know how big a price some people have had to pay for obeying God and following Christ? Read Hebrews 11:35-40. You'll also see that God has a wonderful plan for those who have to take their shots.

THINK ABOUT IT:

When it comes right down to it, what have you actually had to give up for your Christianity? What have you suffered because of Christ? For most of us, the answer is, "Not much."

There are places on this planet where Christians suffer greatly for following Christ, even to the point of death. You might want to say a prayer of thanks that you live in a part of the world where Christianity is more accepted. But ask yourself: In what ways is my faith weaker than it might be if I lived in one of those places where it's dangerous to be a Christian?

THE WORST TRAGEDY

*O*n January 28, 1986, six crew members and one school teacher left a launch pad at Kennedy Space Center aboard the space shuttle Challenger. It was a noteworthy flight for one reason above all: It was the first time a civilian, a non-astronaut, had been included in the crew—a public school teacher, Krista McAuliffe. For that reason, school kids all across the nation, in school and out, had their sets turned on to watch the shuttle launch. You may have been one of them.

Fewer than two minutes into the flight, those thousands of school children, besides the rest of us who had tuned in, watched in shocked disbelief as the space shuttle exploded into a ball of flame. None of us who watched that tragedy will ever forget it.

After my own sorrow and shock had subsided, I wrote down the details of that incident, as well as the emotions and thoughts that it stirred in me. As I wrote, and as I thought about what I had written over the next several months, the directions my thoughts took surprised me.

What I thought was this: As sad and horrible as the Challenger tragedy was, especially for the family and friends of the seven astronauts, there is a worse tragedy that occurs around us every day. Those seven people died at the pinnacle of their careers. They had worked and prepared for that moment for many years, and even though their mission wasn't completed, they had accomplished their part; they had qualified for the mission; they were astronauts. The equipment failure that brought about the explosion wasn't their fault; they died as successes, not failures. Their sacrifices and commitments had propelled them toward the realization of their goals.

Yes, their death, even in that moment of glory, was a national tragedy. But the worse tragedy that surrounds us is the life lived *without* commitment or goals. I'm talking about the aimless souls who find themselves at the end of life without having reached out, without having made peace with God, without having set goals, unable to point back at any accomplishments of significance.

I'm talking, too, about the undisciplined, drunk teenager who drives off the road, dying foolishly in an accident that should never have happened, ending his life before it's hardly begun. Or the sixteen-year-old girl who finds herself pregnant, panics, and ends up before she knows it married to a young man totally unprepared for the responsibilities of family life; that girl suddenly sees her life's options and all her grand hopes and dreams and possibilities narrowed to a few rather unattractive choices.

Those stories are much more tragic than the destruction of the space shuttle Challenger and the seven lives lost that day in 1986.

And those tragedies are not what God wants for us. Not by a long shot. God wants to see us live life to the fullest, at the peak of our potential, and with full-out, one hundred percent effort. He wants that effort to be expended in obedience to him, of course, but don't ever accuse him of wanting us to live quiet, gray, meek little lives.

God is a God of major adventures!

VERSE OF THE DAY:

Do you not know that in a race all the runners run, but only one gets the prize? Run in such a way as to get the prize. Everyone who competes in the games goes into strict training to get a crown that will not last; but we do it to get a crown that will last forever. Therefore I do not run like a man running aimlessly; I do not fight like a man beating the air. No, I beat my body and make it my slave so that after I have preached to others, I myself will not be disqualified for the prize.
—1 Corinthians 9:24-27

HEY!

Read about the great attitude of one who did it right; read 2 Timothy 4:6-8.

JUST DO IT:

How much better it would be to be able to say what the apostle Paul said in today's verse—"I have fought a good fight"—than to have to say, "I gave up."

Or "I never really tried."

Or "I ran at half speed."

On the speedometer shown below, mark the amount of effort you're putting into life. Sure, it's important to play hard, too, but for this exercise I want you to mark the effort you're putting into accomplishing your goals and dreams—not at some pie-in-the-sky level but monthly. In other words, how much effort are you putting *this month* into accomplishing specific goals?

When you've marked your speedometer, it's time to realize that, at whatever level you're now competing in this race, God can take you from there and put you right back into the middle of things—even if you've just been sitting still. After all, you're not racing *against* anyone. You're racing *for* him.

Nobody wants to be thought of as a chicken.

But when Moses was with God up on Mount Sinai, getting the Ten Commandments, there was a great storm on the mountain, with thunder and lightning and smoke and the sound of trumpets. And all the Israelites gathered around the base of the mountain were definitely chicken. The Bible says they "trembled with fear."

"Don't let God come anywhere near us, Moses!" they said. "In fact, don't even let him *talk* to us! Just tell us in your own words what he's saying. Otherwise, we're history."

God wasn't trying to hurt them. In fact, he was trying to help them, but God can seem pretty scary when he's trying to get your attention.

That story, of course, happened a long time ago. But people really haven't changed much. Anytime I'm around a group of teenagers, I know that there'll be many there who've put off even investigating this thing called Christianity, for one reason only: They're afraid.

They say things like, "Man, I don't want to be a Christian. Most of the people I see who claim to be Christians are a bunch of nerds."

That's fear talking, folks. The people who say that are afraid of God. Not in the same way the Israelites were, but there are lots of ways to be afraid of God. The Israelites were afraid that God would kill them, or that his majesty was so great they'd just die if they saw or heard him.

The kids I talk to are afraid of God in a different way. They're afraid because they think God wants to turn them into a big Hostess Twinkie. They think he just wants to destroy their fun—and they're *afraid* of him.

God is powerful. God is awesome. God is holy and strong and just. God *does* want to change our lives; understand that right up front.

And God also loves us. The simple message God sent to those long-ago Israelites through Moses was, "Don't be afraid."

Every time an angel came from God to talk to someone in the Bible, that angel started with these words: "Fear not."

Do these sound like the words of someone we need to fear will hurt us? "Come to me, all you who are weary and burdened, and I will give you rest. Take my yoke upon you and learn from me, for I am gentle and humble in heart, and you will find rest for your souls. For my yoke is easy and my burden is light" (Matt. 11:28-30).

Jesus didn't come to hurt us. He came to give us life and to save us from things that *would* hurt us. We can surrender ourselves to him without fear.

VERSE OF THE DAY:

Therefore Jesus said ..."I have come that they may have life, and have it to the full." —*John 10:7a, 10b.*

HEY!

Want to know what God really has in mind for us? Check out Jeremiah 29:11.

JUST DO IT:

Are *you* afraid of God? Most people are, in one way or another. Maybe you're afraid that if you surrender yourself to him totally, there are things you want to do that he won't want you to. Or maybe he'll want you to do things you aren't capable of. Make a secret list for no one's eyes but your own. Include on it all the things you can think of that you want to do in life—and be honest; include the ones you really don't want to admit to anyone. Then go down the list and ask yourself these questions: *Will being a Christian keep me from doing this? Will I be better off doing this, or not doing this? Is this really going to help me become the kind of adult I want to be?*

When you've gone through your list, ask yourself—Do I really need to be afraid of what effect God will have on my future? Ask God to take away those fears and help you to trust him. You won't be sorry.

PLAYING GAMES WITH GOD

You have to be careful what you pray for. One day I prayed, "Dear God, if you want me to talk about you to someone today, give me a sign."

Later that day I got on a bus, and a dude sat down next to me and started crying. Tears were streaming down his face. After a minute or two he struggled to get himself under control, turned to me and said, "I'm sorry. But my life is just a wreck. Everything that could possibly go wrong has gone wrong. This is the time when I could really use God, but I know absolutely nothing about God." Then he turned to me and asked, "Do *you* know God?"

Know what I did? I said another prayer: "Dear God: Is this a sign? If this is a sign, turn the bus driver into an armadillo."

But hey, don't play games with God! I looked up to the front of the bus, and the bus driver was licking ants off the steering wheel!

Okay, maybe not. But it's true that I was chicken to talk to the guy, and it's true that I played games with God trying to get out of it. There are all kinds of ways to play games with God. Are you ever guilty of any of these?

- Trying to "bargain" with God by telling him that you'll serve him or obey him or do something special for him if he'll just give you what you want?
- Telling him, in some emotional moment like the last night of camp or at a revival service, that you're going to change and be a super-Christian, only to go right back to the same old life by the end of the week?
- Avoiding something you know you should do by rationalizing it away with some silly argument you know isn't true? (Such as: "God couldn't want me to obey my dad and clean my room right now, because it's Sunday afternoon—God doesn't want us to work on Sundays!")
- Blaming God for things you really know aren't his fault so you won't feel as guilty about disobeying him?

Let's play fair with God. Let's do what we say we're going to do. After all, God isn't somebody to fool around with. If he can turn a bus driver into an armadillo ...

Okay, forget the armadillo. We don't play games with God, because he's the one who made us, who made the whole universe, who died for us on the cross.

We don't play games with God because he *is* God.

VER/E OF THE DAY:
Do not be deceived: God cannot be mocked. A man reaps what he sows.
—Galatians 6:7

HEY!
Want to know why it's impossible to fool God? Read Luke 16:13-15.

JU/T DO IT:
"God knows your hearts," says Jesus in Luke 16:15. That means he knows even our thoughts—and it's hard to play games with someone who knows what you're thinking. Even so, we all try it.

Try to figure out at least one way in which you're playing games with God right now—maybe something you're doing that you really know is wrong but that you're rationalizing is okay, maybe some promise you made to God that you're trying to wriggle out of. Then come up with a plan for making it right, for ending the games.

I was almost flunking out of Oak Hills Bible College when a professor called me into his office. At first, he just chatted—then he leaned across the desk and asked a question that no one had ever asked me before: "What do you dream of becoming?"

I had to think about it, but finally I stammered out the list of ambitious goals I'd like to achieve in life.

"Why, then," he asked, "when you have such admirable goals, do you live with this kind of mediocrity?" He slid my midterm grades across the desk, and my face reddened. They were not a pretty sight. I tried to choke out some reasonable excuse, but he cut me off with these words: "You say you aspire to excellence, yet you settle for mediocrity." He tapped those horrible grades with his finger. I have never forgotten what he said next. "Ken, it is not what a person dreams that determines what he will become. It is what a person does every day of his life." Then came the necessary encouragement: "I believe you are capable of all you have dreamed, Ken. Why don't you start living as though *you* believe it?"

WHAT IS YOUR DREAM?

I graduated near the top of my class.

What are your dreams? When you lie in bed at night, in those quiet moments before you fall asleep, do you think about what life might hold for you and what you'd like to do? Maybe you think about becoming a pilot, or a dancer, or a major-league pitcher, or an actor, or the head of a big corporation. Maybe you think about having children, or maybe you want to be a missionary and carry God's Word to those who've never heard it.

Terrific dreams. But they will never become reality unless you start living as if those goals are important and worth working for. God has created each of us with remarkable abilities, but it is up to us to develop and use them wisely.

And you can't wait until you're on the verge of accomplishing your dream to begin that process. It begins now. Or you may one day see your dreams slipping away.

It is not what you dream that determines what you will become. It is what you do, every day of your life.

VERSE OF THE DAY:

Do your best to present yourself to God as one approved, a workman who does not need to be ashamed and who correctly handles the word of truth.

—2 Timothy 2:15

HEY!

Want the list of things it takes to accomplish your dreams? Read 2 Peter 1:5-9.

JUST DO IT:

What are your dreams? Identify two or three things you would like to accomplish in your life. What should you be doing now to prepare yourself to accomplish those goals when the time comes? Maybe you should be working harder in school, or keeping yourself in good physical shape and eating right, or working harder at developing good social skills, such as meeting people or carrying on a conversation. If you aren't sure what you need to be doing now, think of someone who might be able to help you figure that out and find the time to ask that person for some help.

Just about everybody knows the story of Jonah—how he ran away when God told him to go to Nineveh and preach to the sinful people there, and how the sailors threw him overboard during a great storm, and how a fish swallowed him up for three days and then spat him out on the land, all bleached out and smelling like whale barf.

RUNNING FROM GOD

If you *aren't* familiar with the story, take a few minutes to read it right now in the book of Jonah, chapters 1 through 4—it isn't long.

But despite all of those exciting and bizarre parts of the story, the part that haunts me is just a tiny little part near the beginning. When Jonah decided to run from God, he ran down to the docks, paid the fare, and shipped out on a boat bound for a place called Tarshish. A violent storm came up, and the sailors were afraid that the ship would break up and they'd die at sea.

Where was Jonah while they were trying to save the ship? He had gone down below deck and fallen into a deep sleep.

A deep sleep? Are you kidding? This man is running from a mighty God, trying to avoid what God commanded him to do. He should be sitting in the corner, biting his fingernails. Instead, he's sleeping so soundly that even a great storm doesn't wake him up.

I find that a scary thought. There are lots of dangers in running from God, but Jonah doesn't seem to be aware of them. He is ignoring God. And that may be the worst danger of all.

At your age, your spirit is still moldable and soft. The cement of your being has not yet set. Statistics tell us that most of the people who make the wise and eternal decision to follow Christ do it before the age of eighteen; after that age, the likelihood of deciding to follow Christ diminishes rapidly. Why? Because we've become hardened in our ways. We find it easy to sleep through God's loving call to us.

That's why the Bible tells us, "Remember your creator in the days of your youth" (Ecclesiastes 12:1).

If we turn our backs on God, will he stop pursuing us? Will he stop calling to us, whispering his message to us in the quiet hours? No, he will continue. His love compels him to. But the longer you run from him, the easier you will find it to shut him out until finally, even while he pleads with you, you'll find it possible to slip into the bottom of the ship and drown yourself in some kind of sleep.

And then you won't hear him anymore—not because he's stopped loving you, and not because he's stopped calling, but because you've hardened yourself toward him to the point that you no longer hear him.

Like Jonah.

VERSE OF THE DAY:

For this people's heart has become calloused; they hardly hear with their ears, and they have closed their eyes. Otherwise they might see with their eyes, hear with their ears, understand with their hearts and turn, and I would heal them.
—Acts 28:27

HEY!

Want to know why it's dangerous to ignore God? Find out in Hebrews 3:7-19.

JUST DO IT:

Okay, maybe you're not Jonah sleeping in the hold of a ship out on the Mediterranean, but there are probably certain areas of your life you're withholding from God—things he's trying to talk to you about, but you refuse to hear his voice. On a secret piece of paper that no one but you will see, write down what a couple of those things are. That's your "Nineveh." You're running away from God's will in that area. On the rest of that sheet of paper, write a prayer and tell God what you plan to do about it.

Y ou can get well from a number of things. You can get well from mononucleosis. You can get well from the flu, from spinal meningitis, from the measles—you can even get well from cancer most of the time.

"I DIED FRIDAY."

But you won't hear very many people saying, "Yeah, I died Friday—but I'm feeling better today."

Death is one thing you don't get well from. Death is permanent.

That's why it's so surprising in the book of John, chapter 11, when Jesus says of his friend Lazarus, "'This sickness will not end in death .... Lazarus has fallen asleep; but I am going there to wake him up'" (vv. 4 and 11).

Lazarus isn't asleep. He's dead! And Jesus knows he's dead, because he says so just three verses later. So why does he say that his friend is only asleep? Because Jesus *is* going there to wake him up—from the dead.

Contrary to what we think, death is not the end, and Jesus knew that. He wanted to demonstrate that truth to his disciples and his followers in a way they'd never forget (speaking for myself, if I saw somebody raised from the dead, I know I'd never forget it!)—and he wanted them to know that he is powerful even over death.

"This sickness will not end in death," he said.

We're all suffering from a variety of problems that seem very serious to us—and many of them are. For some of us, it's a problem with a girlfriend or boyfriend. Or a problem at school, or a problem with money. Some are depressed—*really* depressed. Others wonder whether their families will stay together long enough for them to graduate from high school. Some have made some bad decisions that are hurting them now. Some are fighting serious illnesses. And some have more serious problems even than that.

And we often get so discouraged that we think that even God can't do anything about those problems, they seem so serious to us.

God *can't* do anything about our problems? The God who created the universe, not to mention first raising Lazarus and then Jesus from the dead? That's the thing I love about this passage of

Scripture—it reminds me that, no matter how serious my problems are, Lazarus had a worse one. He had what you might call a permanent disability. He was *dead!* In fact, he'd been dead four days! And Jesus raised him up.

God has never promised to heal every sickness or make all the hurts go away. He has promised to help us face even the toughest problems. Most of us think of dying as the biggest problem we could ever face—but Jesus' death and resurrection defeated even death.

The next time you feel that he isn't big enough to help with the problem you're facing, just remember Lazarus. Even death won't end in death. And the one who defeated death is available to help you today.

VERSE OF THE DAY:

"Death has been swallowed up in victory. Where, O death, is your victory? Where, O death, is your sting?" ... But thanks be to God! He gives us the victory through our Lord Jesus Christ. —1 Corinthians 15:54-55, 57

HEY!

Is Jesus really powerful enough to do all that stuff and to keep all his promises? Read Ephesians 1:18-23.

JUST DO IT:

What things would you do differently in your life if you *really, really* believe that Jesus is as mighty as the Bible says he is? Make a list of those things. Now make another list—of the reasons that you aren't doing the things on the first list. Is the list of reasons on the second list more important than a God who can overcome death?

Now go *live* as though you believe!

We're not used to looking for humor in the things that Jesus said, but sometimes he uncorked a good one.

ONE STRUNG-OUT CAMEL

Once a rich young man came to talk to Jesus; you can read about it in Matthew 19:16—26. First he asked Jesus what he needed to do to earn eternal life, and Jesus told him to obey all the commandments.

"I've done that," the young man said.

"Then go and sell everything you own," Jesus answered him, "and give the money to the poor. Then come and follow me."

But the man couldn't bring himself to do that because he was so rich. So as the young man walked away, Jesus turned to his disciples and said, "It is easier for a camel to go through the eye of a needle than for a rich man to enter the kingdom of God" (Matt. 19:24).

What a comment! I get incredible mental pictures when I read that verse. I mean, how would you get a camel through the eye of your typical sewing needle? Would you start with the tail, licking the end and twisting it to get a fine point? Would you tug with all your strength trying to get the rest of him to follow?

And if you *did* get that camel through that little hole, just imagine how he'd look. That would be one strung-out camel!

Believe it or not, there are Bible scholars who debate about how it might be possible to get that camel through the eye of the needle. They argue that there was a tiny gate in the Jerusalem city wall that might have been called the Eye of the Needle because it was so hard to get through, and that, just maybe, you really *could* get that camel through that gate if you stripped his saddle off and got him down on his knees and ...

Maybe they're missing the point. Maybe Jesus was just trying to get across the idea to his disciples that it was so hard for a rich man to go to heaven that it might as well be impossible—like stringing a camel through a needle's eye. Nowadays we might say something like: "It's harder than pushing a worm through a straw."

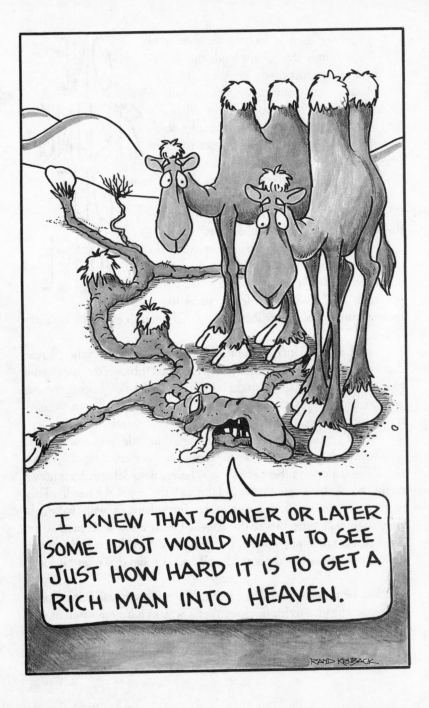

The disciples knew Jesus well enough to get the point. They knew that he was talking about something impossible. After they finished laughing (Ken Davis version of the Bible), they said, "Who then can be saved?" (Matt. 19:25).

And I love Jesus' answer: "With man this is impossible, but with God all things are possible" (Matt. 19:26).

Isn't that great? No matter how far removed from God someone is, or how reluctant to leave behind the things that stand between him and God, God's love can still reach that person. Maybe it's money that's standing between you and God. Maybe it's drugs, or a low self-image, or anger, or pride, or lust. Whatever it is, God can break through it. You might not be able to on your own, but God can.

With God, all things are possible.

But I'd still like to see that snapshot of the camel right after he comes through the eye of the needle—long, stringy, and hurtin' real bad.

VERSE OF THE DAY:

Jesus looked at them and said, "With man this is impossible, but with God all things are possible."
—Matthew 19:26

HEY!

Read Luke 12:15-21. Be cool—don't be a fool.

JUST DO IT:

What things come between you and God most often? A relationship? A possession? A position of authority? Your love for money, or status, or something else?

God can break through that—but not if you walk away sadly, like that rich young man in the story above. You need to take it to him.

Write out a prayer in which you present to God the area of your life that seems to be coming between you and him, and ask him to help you set that aside. Then pray the prayer you've written.

Keep that prayer to remind yourself of what you've asked God to do.

DOES JESUS WORK AT YOUR HOUSE?

When I'm out on the road speaking, I hear nothing but praise.

"Ken, you're so funny!"

"Ken, you've helped me so much. My life will never be the same."

"Ken, we've had a lot of speakers here, but no one has held our attention or made us laugh like this before."

And I get great reviews in the press. "Great Comedian!" "A very funny man!" And that's where the problem arises: I start to believe my own press clippings. *Hey, I'm pretty great!*

And then I come home. After spending several days with people who've only seen me at my best, suddenly I'm with the people who see the rest of me. And who don't mind telling me so. Wife and kids both. Sometimes it's enough to make me want to head back out on the road!

But that's all right. Because I know that it isn't enough to be a Christian when I'm with a bunch of people I've just met and probably won't see again for a while. I've got to be a Christian at home, too. And if Jesus doesn't work at home, he doesn't work anywhere.

So coming home is my reality check. How is my Christianity working? And my family isn't afraid to tell me. And even if I don't always like what I hear, I *want* them to tell me.

It doesn't matter if you're the president of your youth group, it doesn't matter if you can give a wonderful testimony that brings tears to everyone's eyes—if your Christianity isn't working at home, it isn't working.

When I was a teenager, I wasn't usually very happy with the way things were going in my house. But during the entire time I lived at home, I didn't spend five minutes thinking about what I could do to make life more pleasant for the rest of the people living in that house. My Christianity wasn't working. Or maybe I should say: I wasn't working my Christianity. And it wasn't God's fault.

Are you working your Christianity? Are you working it at home?

VERSE OF THE DAY:

If anyone says, "I love God," yet hates his brother, he is a liar. For anyone who does not love his brother, whom he has seen, cannot love God, whom he has not seen.
— *1 John 4:20*

HEY!

If you think you have it bad at home, you ought to read about somebody who really had things rough—his brothers tried to kill him! But he still loved them and forgave them. Read about Joseph in Genesis 37-45 and 50:15-21. (I know, I know—that's a lot of reading. But it's a fascinating story! Read it over a few days.)

JUST DO IT:

If you're going to make some changes in the way you live as a Christian at home, you need a plan. Write down your plan in four columns: What changes you want to make; what effect on your family you hope that change will have; how you're going to make that change; and a date by which you want to have that change fully accomplished. (The date is important because sometimes those changes don't come overnight. It takes time to change habits.)

When you've made that list, ask God for the power to make those changes—for the power to work your Christianity at home.

Want some other ideas? Read Ken's book *How to Live with Your Parents Without Losing Your Mind*, also published by Zondervan.

WHO SHOUTS THE LOUDEST?

Years ago I tried an experiment with a hundred college students in an auditorium at Rockford College. In the first phase of this three-phase experiment, we took a volunteer from the auditorium into another room, where he was blindfolded and told that when he returned he could do anything he wanted. Meanwhile, the rest of the students were told to individually think of a simple task—*any* simple task—that the volunteer could do inside the auditorium and to shout those instructions to him when he came back into the room.

But one of those students received very special instructions. He was to shout to the blindfolded volunteer to walk to the back of the auditorium, climb the steps, and embrace a faculty member who was waiting there. And he was to shout those instructions as if it were a matter of life and death. We called his message the "vital message."

The results were predictable. When the blindfolded volunteer was led back into the auditorium, the room exploded with shouts. No single voice or message stood out; the vital message was lost in the din. The blindfolded student stood a while in confusion and indecision and then began to move about randomly, without purpose, trying to discern one clear and unmistakable voice in the crowd.

We sent the volunteer from the room and gave instructions for phase two. In this phase, the student who had been shouting the vital message was told that he could get out of his seat. But another student was given a conflicting task: to persuade the blindfolded volunteer *not* to go to the back of the room and embrace the faculty member. These two students were told that they could stand as close to the blindfolded volunteer as they wished, without touching him, to shout their opposing messages.

The volunteer was led back into the room, and the shouting began again. This time, besides the general uproar in the room, there were two closer, louder voices—shouting opposing messages. The blindfolded student would obey first one of those voices, then the other. He shuffled toward the back of the room and then, persuaded by the other voice, turned and shuffled back toward the front only to turn again a moment or two later.

We sent him from the room again and gave instructions for phase three. The situation was the same as in phase two—*except that this time the student with the vital message was allowed to touch the blindfolded student.* He was not allowed to pull, push, or in any way force the volunteer to do his bidding, but he could touch him.

The volunteer was led back in, and the earsplitting shouting began again. The two messengers stood close, shouting their opposing words. Then, the one with the vital message put his arm gently around the volunteer's shoulder and leaned very close to speak directly into his ear. Almost without hesitation, the volunteer began to yield to his instruction. Occasionally he paused to listen as the opposing messenger frantically tried to persuade him to turn around. But always, the gentle touch of the one with the vital message led him on.

Then something unforeseen happened. As the blindfolded student drew close to his goal, the students in the auditorium who, up to this point, had been shouting their own individual instructions, suddenly joined in unison to keep the volunteer from taking those final steps! "Don't go! Don't go! Don't go!" they chanted, louder and louder.

But the guiding arm of the messenger never left the shoulder of the volunteer, and when they reached the top of the stairs at the back of the auditorium, the messenger leaned over to whisper his final instructions. There was a moment of hesitation, and then the volunteer threw his arms around the faculty member, and the auditorium erupted in cheers and applause. And, not surprisingly—because it was an emotional exercise—there were more than a few damp eyes in the room.

Asked later why he had followed the one with the vital message, the one who had touched him, the volunteer replied, "Because it felt like he was the only one who really cared."

I will never forget that experiment. It illustrated more clearly than anything I've heard or seen since how we can affect the behavior and even beliefs of those we love when we see them entering dangerous territory. We don't do it by shouting from the sidelines or from the safety of our seats in the auditorium; we don't do it by frantically yelling instructions in their ears; we don't do it by multiplying the voices they hear shouting at them. We do it by walking alongside, communicating our love and care through our lives, and sharing in words that can be as gentle as a whisper. We do it not by our persuasive arguments but by our touch.

VERSE OF THE DAY:

"A new command I give you: Love one another. As I have loved you, so you must love one another." —John 13:34

HEY!

Here's a great example of loving concern — showing our love by our actions: Luke 10:25-37.

JUST DO IT:

Not long ago I sat with a girl who wept with concern over her sister, who was heading for a life of rebellion and anger and lack of self-control. "What can I do to help her?" she asked.

She had tried all the arguments. She had even tried shaming her sister. Nothing had worked. And now she felt like giving up.

Do you have a friend whose actions and decisions concern you, or a friend you would like to see trust Christ? Reread today's story and write down a few ideas for how you can make a difference in that friend's life. (Hint: When God tried to reach us, how did he do it? Preach? Yell? And did he ever give up? What act of love finally broke through?)

Do you think God ever had reason to give up on you? Why didn't he? Why won't he? Reread today's verse and think of some way you can let your friend know how much you care.

By the way—I told that girl who was worried about her sister to simply *love* that sister. "Is that all I can do?" she asked.

"It's more than that," I answered. "It's the *best* you can do."

TOUGH SHEEP

Picture a bunch of little sheep running down the valley. One little sheep is trailing behind; he weighs all of about twenty-five pounds. Up on the hill, behind a rock, hides a lion. He's a hungry lion; he hasn't eaten for three-and-a-half years. He's not looking for puppy chow. He's looking for lamb.

The lion sees that little lamb, and he leaps out from behind the rock and roars down the hill, his claws ripping up big chunks of turf. Saliva drips from his jaws, his huge mane is blowing in the wind, and he hits the valley floor and leaps for that little sheep.

The sheep turns around and sees that huge lion in the air, jaws wide open, coming down on him.

That sheep has two options.

Option one: Fight.

Wouldn't that be great? Here's a little twenty-five pound sheep strutting back and forth, saying, "I'm ba-a-a-ad! Come on! You wanta get down? Okay, let's rumble! I'm ba-a-a-a! Ba-a-a-a! Ba-a-a-ad!"

I can just see the lion stop in mid-air, take one look at that woolly geek, and say, "No way! I don't want no part of that!"

Okay, I agree. Not too likely. So that sheep better examine option two: Run to the shepherd.

The Bible says, "Your enemy the devil prowls around like a roaring lion looking for someone to devour" (1 Peter 5:8). And we're out there like a bunch of sheep!

The prognosis is not good—unless you take that little sheep and put him with the shepherd. Then do you know what you get?

Super sheep.

And you, too, can be a super sheep. But not on your own. On your own you're lion bait.

VERSE OF THE DAY:

Even though I walk
 through the valley of the shadow of death,
I will fear no evil,
 for you are with me.

— *Psalm 23:4*

HEY!

For a sheep's-eye view of the shepherd, read the rest of Psalm 23. And to find out what a real shepherd does for his sheep, read John 10:11-15.

JUST DO IT:

If you've never done it before, today is a good day to put your trust in the shepherd who gave his life for you—Jesus Christ. Then you, too, can be a super sheep.

How do you do that? Just say a simple prayer, something like this: "Dear God, I know that because I've sinned, I can't come up to your standards. And I also know that your Son, Jesus, died on the cross to pay the penalty for my sins so that I could have a relationship with you. So I accept the gift you're offering me: a relationship with you and with your son, Jesus, now—and eternal life with you after I die. I want to be part of your family. Thank you for accepting me! Amen."

Did you pray that prayer? Now you're a super sheep, too! Write down today's date on the bottom of this page so that you can remember when you became a super sheep—and a Christian.

THE POW

My father was a prisoner of war, living near starvation, for three-and-a-half years. His waking hours were completely taken up with finding and hoarding food. Rotten rice and even insects were hidden—saved to be eaten later when hunger could no longer be ignored.

When his prison camp was liberated, planes flew over and dropped barrels full of food. One of those barrels landed in front of my father and broke open—scattering hundreds of candy bars on the ground in front of the starving prisoners. Surprisingly, few of those prisoners ate them immediately. Instead, they gathered as many as they could and stuffed them into their tattered clothing for later. Every one of those men knew that the war was over and that relief was already arriving, yet they couldn't break the hoarding habit they had developed over years of imprisonment.

What's the point of that story? How neat it would be if a plane dropped a barrelful of candy bars in front of you so you could start stuffing them into every pocket? Not quite. The point is that, once we've established a habit, it becomes very difficult to break—even when the habit makes absolutely no sense anymore. Even when the habit is hurting us.

We all have habits. There are even habits that aren't necessarily harmful, such as which breakfast cereal you habitually eat, or how you put your makeup on in the morning. Then there are habits that aren't specifically sinful but definitely harmful, such as poor study habits. Then there are sinful habits, such as substance abuse or overeating (yes, friends, that *is* a sin), or treating the people around us poorly.

Any of those habits would be hard to break because we are indeed creatures of habit. But those habits that are hurting us or hurting those around us need to be broken.

And the longer you wait to break those harmful habits, the harder it will be.

VERSE OF THE DAY:

Therefore do not let sin reign in your mortal body so that you obey its evil desires. Do not offer the parts of your body to sin, as instruments of wickedness, but rather offer yourselves to God. —Romans 6:12, 13

HEY!

Want to know what one of the best reasons is for breaking bad habits? You'll find it in Hebrews 12:1-3.

JUST DO IT:

If you read Hebrews 12:1-3, you found out that one of the crucial steps in "running the race" God has marked out for us—in other words, living the Christian life victoriously—is "throwing off everything that hinders and the sin that so easily entangles." Bad habits definitely qualify as something that hinders and entangles.

How about you? Are you dealing with habits that are destructive or sinful? Be honest. If the answer is yes, then talk about it to someone you can trust. Don't give in to bad habits and don't give up, either. With God's help and maybe with some counseling, you can defeat bad habits and learn new ways to live.

*O*ne Sunday morning when my daughter Taryn was small, we were sitting in church. Everyone was facing the front, of course, as people do in church—everyone, that is, except for Taryn, who was standing on the pew facing backward, grinning at everyone behind us and reporting on what she saw. During a silent moment of prayer, she whispered loudly enough for the whole church to hear: "That lady doesn't have her eyes closed!" I could hear muffled laughter everywhere.

"**YOU SMELL LIKE DEAD ROSES!**"

As the prayer ended, Taryn turned to the lady sitting next to her and said, "You know what?"

Okay, let's pause here so I can tell you something: When you get married and have kids and you're out in public with those kids and one of them says, "You know what?"— shut her up quickly. Whatever it takes—clamp a hand around their mouth, stick a cork in them, whatever it takes—don't let them tell "what."

Once more, the whole church heard my child say, "You know what?" I dived for her, but I didn't make it in time. She said to that lady, "You know what? You smell real bad."

Now I had a problem. That lady was ticked off. The rest of the congregation was rolling on the floor because they knew it was true!

"You don't talk like that to people," I whispered hoarsely as I pulled Taryn into my lap.

"Well, it's the truth," she shouted back.

"Then don't tell the truth," I whispered back through clenched teeth.

"You want me to lie?"

I can just hear her the next time: "You know what? You smell like a vase of roses. *Dead* roses. Roses that have been dead a *long time.*"

Little kids will lie to get what they want or to protect themselves from getting into trouble; we all know that. But other than that, they usually tell the truth even when it hurts.

Now, I'm not suggesting that you encourage your children to be odor sheriffs, bent on verbally identifying all the stinkers in your church. But the simple fact is that sometimes the truth hurts. If you're to grow as a Christian, you must be open to allowing God (sometimes through others) to identify areas of your life that might not be pleasantly fragrant (and some areas that may smell like roadkill) so that he can use his Spirit to empower you to change.

I know that sounds hard, but don't worry—it's even harder than it sounds. Even so, just remember: Once you've identified the areas of your life that smell real bad, God can sweeten them up. And that is something you will never regret.

VERSE OF THE DAY:

Search me, O God, and know my heart;
test me and know my anxious thoughts.
See if there is any offensive way in me;
and lead me in the way everlasting.   —Psalm 139:23, 24

HEY!

Another great psalm about being cleansed by God is Psalm 51:1-15. Read it carefully and notice that the psalmist doesn't waste any time defending himself. He knows that all of him needs renewal and cleansing.

JUST DO IT:

Read today's verse again, as a prayer—a sincere prayer. Then watch how God answers that prayer. If you find out some things about yourself you don't like, the truth may hurt momentarily. But in the end, you'll smell a whole lot better.

JESUS WEPT

When I was a kid, we could earn our way to camp by memorizing verses. That's why I loved the shortest verse in the Bible, John 11:35: "Jesus wept." Two words. Took me only two or three days to memorize that verse.

But I never really understood it. Jesus wept? Why would Jesus weep?

So one day I asked a man I knew, and he put his arm around my shoulders and said, "Well, Ken, remember: when Jesus said that, he was at the funeral of his friend Lazarus. Jesus was as human as you or I, and like anyone else at a funeral, he was saddened by the death of his friend."

I believed that explanation. At least, I believed it until I read the Scripture for myself. And when I read it for myself, I found some problems with that explanation.

For one thing, Jesus was planning to raise Lazarus from the dead. If he was planning to raise his friend from the dead, why would he weep over his death?

For another, Jesus specifically told the disciples that he was glad he hadn't been there to heal Lazarus before he died, so that they could see the miracle that would strengthen their faith. Why would he weep if he was glad for the opportunity to demonstrate his power to his disciples?

But why, then, *did* Jesus weep?

I think the answer to that question is in the response Jesus got when he and his disciples arrived at Bethany to raise Lazarus to life again. "'Lord, if you had been here, my brother would not have died.'"

They didn't believe that he could—or would—raise Lazarus from the dead! Not even when he told them that's what he planned to do. Yes, Martha replied, she knew that Lazarus would rise again—"'in the resurrection at the last day.'" But Jesus wanted to do it now!

They didn't understand the wonderful gift that he was offering to them! And the Bible says that when Jesus heard that evidence of their unbelief and saw them still weeping in grief when he came to bring them joy instead, "he was deeply moved in spirit and troubled ... Jesus wept."

He wept because the people he loved were in intense pain and couldn't see that he wanted to take away the cause of that pain.

Are there times when you're so loaded down with pain or frustration or anger or sadness or loneliness that you can't understand or accept what God is offering you? Whatever it is, it can't be any worse than Martha's loss of her brother. If Jesus could raise Lazarus from the dead—and he did—then he can handle whatever problems I'm facing, and he can handle whatever problems you're facing.

What brings sorrow to our Lord is when we can't see what he offers and we don't take advantage of his power. What brings joy to him is when we see what he offers and we respond with our lives, allowing him to bring us the abundance and joy he promised.

VERSE OF THE DAY:

Jesus said to her, "I am the resurrection and the life. He who believes in me will live, even though he dies; and whoever lives and believes in me will never die. Do you believe this?" —John 11:25, 26

HEY!

You can read the whole story of Lazarus's death and resurrection in John 11:1-45.

JUST DO IT:

We think it's sad, when we read the story of Lazarus, that some of Jesus' closest friends didn't have enough faith in him to believe that he could do what he said. But those friends, such as Mary and Martha, were no different from the rest of us. Each of us has areas of need that we really haven't turned over to Jesus yet, despite the fact that he wants so badly to help us with those areas. What troubled areas of your life have you never really turned over to Christ yet? How will you go about doing that?

SEATBELTS OF THE HEART

In one of my favorite stories, a little girl was misbehaving on a commercial airliner, running up and down the aisles and disturbing the passengers. Several times the harried mother went after her daughter and brought her back to her seat only to see her squirt out of it a moment or two later and resume her mischief. Finally, because the little girl had been harassing an impatient businessman, the stewardess brought her back to her mother. "You need to keep your daughter seated," the stewardess insisted.

The mother roughly pushed the little girl into her seat, snapped the seatbelt tightly around her, and hissed through clenched teeth, "Now you sit!"

The little girl obediently sat with her arms folded and an impish smile on her face.

"Why are you smiling?" the angry mother snapped.

"Because," the little girl smirked, "I may be sittin' on the outside, but on the inside I'm still jumpin' around."

The seatbelt could only restrain her body; it couldn't change the little girl's heart.

What a truth—and I'll bet it's a truth you can identify with. Ever been in a situation where you were forced to be quiet and respectful when inside you felt angry or rebellious? Or, worse yet, have you ever been in a situation where there *was* no seatbelt—where no one would ever know if you misbehaved?

In those situations, it isn't the rules that rule. It's the heart that rules. When there's no one around to enforce them, rules mean nothing unless they are *your* rules, coming from your heart. The rules your parents make are sometimes broken when your parents aren't around and you think they won't find out. Rules you're given at church might be broken when you're somewhere else and no one from your church would ever know. But heartrules—rules you adopt yourself, rules you believe in, rules from the heart—are seldom broken.

Outside rules, those that are imposed on you by parents, or church, or someone else, operate on the principle, "I can't—or I'll get in trouble." Heartrules operate on this principle: "I don't want to."

Whose rules are you following?

VERSE OF THE DAY:

But Daniel resolved not to defile himself with the royal food and wine, and he asked the chief official for permission not to defile himself this way. —Daniel 1:8

HEY!

Read the rest of the story of Daniel and the king's food and wine in Daniel 1.

JUST DO IT:

If you haven't read Daniel 1 yet, you're probably still wondering what today's verse, Daniel 1:8, has to do with seatbelts and heartrules. So read that chapter right now.

Now do you see? Daniel didn't refuse to eat the king's food just because some religious leaders had made a rule or because his mother told him never to eat it. He resolved in his own heart that he wouldn't defile his body in that way even though he could easily have been killed for defying the king's orders. He stood firmly. He followed his own heartrule.

List some of the rules in your life. Which ones are heartrules? Which ones are merely seatbelts? Make sure that the ones that count are from the heart, rules you'll follow even when it's tough, even when there's nobody there to know.

HANDKERCHIEFS, FINGERNAILS, AND SUNDAY SCHOOL

A mom I met from Louisiana was shocked when her seven-year-old son, Carson, announced, "I'm not going to church anymore. Ever."

She launched into a long, impassioned lecture about the importance of going to church, then finally paused long enough to ask Carson why he didn't want to go.

"Because it's stupid," he responded.

She checked her impulse to scold him angrily for being disrespectful and asked instead, "Why do you think it's stupid?"

His answer astounded her: "Because of the handkerchiefs." Every Sunday, he explained, the teacher would check to see which children were "good citizens." Fingernails and ears were inspected to see whether they were clean, the children were asked whether they had brushed their teeth, and each one had to show that he had a clean handkerchief. Carson didn't own a handkerchief and was embarrassed to ask his parents to get him one. Every Sunday the kids who passed inspection would receive little stars they could paste on a paper crown—their reward for being good citizens. Carson's crown was empty.

And Carson was right—this *was* stupid. Every Sunday, regardless of the good intentions of the teacher, Carson was facing unnecessary embarrassment.

Carson's wise mom presented him with a bright white handkerchief with his initials in the corner and the reassurance that he was a good citizen whether he carried it or not. She then tactfully helped the teacher to understand the emotional consequences of this little exercise. And Carson no longer wants to skip church.

But maybe you do. And just maybe your reasons for not enjoying church are, in the end, very much like Carson's. Not that somebody's waiting to inspect your fingernails and ears and check your handkerchief. (Gross!) But there may have been sometime in your past a Sunday school teacher, or a parent, or a pastor, or somebody who had less interest in *you* than in how you dressed or acted or talked, and who made you feel unloved and unwelcome.

And now, just maybe, you remember that person with bitterness and sometimes don't want to go to church at all. Because it seems stupid.

Please remember one thing: Church is *God's* house. He invites us to come and spend some time with him each week, and it's a mistake to let anybody else scare us away. Sure, it's tempting to just say, *I'll skip the church service—it's full of hypocrites anyway. I'll stay home and read my Bible and pray.* It's a good thing to read your Bible and pray at home, but today's verse says that isn't enough.

Don't let somebody else's mistakes stand between you and God.

VERSE OF THE DAY:

Let us not give up meeting together, as some are in the habit of doing, but let us encourage one another. —Hebrews 10:25

HEY!

Want to know what the very first churches were like? Read Acts 2:42-47, and find out why so many people joined up. One thing for sure, they weren't boring!

JUST DO IT:

Find a few minutes today to remember some of your unpleasant memories of church: a harsh teacher or pastor, boredom, being made to feel foolish—anything that might make you uneasy about going back to church. When you've remembered a couple of incidents, talk it over with a friend, or parent, or youth pastor—sometimes just sharing those unpleasant experiences helps! Then, next time you go to church, make a couple of adjustments:

1. Ask God to give you a specific challenge through your experience there;

2. Find someone to reach out to—a newcomer to make feel welcome, friends to greet, someone to say hi to, someone to make feel loved.

Remember—church is never fun as a spectator sport. Dive in and get involved!

THE CURE

A friend of mine died a few years ago from cancer. I only wish I had had the cure! Then I could have saved him.

Imagine that as he was dying, I had been able to run into his hospital room and say, "Here it is—this is the cure! I've found it! This will eliminate your cancer, and you can live. It has worked for others, and it will work for you. You don't have to die!"

Now imagine how I'd have felt if my friend, dying in his bed, turned to me and said, "No, thanks."

"What! Maybe you didn't understand. This will *cure* you."

"I understood you. It's just that most of my friends think this cure is a big joke, and if I take it—well, I'm afraid of what they'll think of me. I'll just stick with the cancer."

Every week I meet young people who, deep in their hearts, understand that Jesus Christ has offered us the cure for our loneliness and depression and sin. They also understand that when they turn their backs on Christ, they are turning their backs on that cure. But they turn their backs anyway. Why? Not because they're cool. Not because they're tough. But because they're afraid of what their friends will think.

I also see those who are already Christians live and speak in ways that they know aren't pleasing to God, but that they think will please their friends. Why? You've got it—they care more about what their friends think than they do about what God thinks. If we're going to be honest, I think we'll have to admit that we all do this sometimes, kids and adults alike. I've been caught in this trap more than once.

There's a powerful scene in David Wilkerson's book *The Cross and the Switchblade.* Wilkerson speaks at a big rally to which he has invited all the gangs he's been witnessing to for several weeks. At the end, he asks all those who want to accept God's cure to come to the front, and several stand to come forward.

But immediately, their friends begin ridiculing them.

"Do you really *believe* that stuff? It's stupid!"

"You go up there, you're out of the gang!"

Girls said to their boyfriends, "Sit back down or I'm through with you!"

And some of those kids listened to those voices and went back to their seats. Others listened to what God was saying and went to the front of the auditorium to take the cure.

Your friends can help you know what clothes are cool, they can help you study, they can keep you from feeling lonely, they can help you feel that you belong. But only you can decide about your relationship with God.

Don't let your friends make that choice for you.

VERSE OF THE DAY:

Do not follow the crowd in doing wrong. — *Exodus 23:2*

HEY!

Remember: you really have to think about who you're choosing as friends. To find out why, read 1 Corinthians 15:33 and Psalm 1:1, 2.

JUST DO IT:

Think for a few minutes about how your friends have influenced your relationship with God. Have they encouraged you in that relationship? Discouraged you? Ridiculed you? Which friends have had a positive influence on your Christianity, and which have had a negative influence?

Don't be afraid to stand up for what you believe. You may find out who your *real* friends are.

WHO'S THAT WALKING ON THE WATER?

Picture this: A boatful of fishermen on the Sea of Galilee; it's night, the water is rough, and the wind is strong. Spray from the waves that crash against the boat soak the worried fishermen.

One of the men—Peter, the disciple—strains against his oar. He wipes the water out of his eyes and scans the darkness for a light, or any sign that they're approaching land. Suddenly he sees a movement out in the waves. Another boat? A rock? A piece of wreckage from a boat capsized in the storm? He squints and watches—there it is again! And this time it looks almost like a person. He wipes the spray from his eyes again and takes another look. Amazingly, beyond belief, he sees that it *is* a person—walking on the water!

How would Peter—or anyone else—respond to that? Would he yawn, "Lo, verily, someone walketh upon the water"?

Are you kidding? I imagine he yelled like crazy: "Bringeth me the binoculars!"

Okay, Peter didn't have binoculars, but it's obvious that he and the rest of the crew went ballistic with excitement and fear. They probably almost tipped the boat over as they pressed against the rail for a better look.

And the Bible says that then the disciples cried out in fear, "Yipes!" (KDV—Ken Davis version.) "It's a ghost!" (NIV)

"Don't be afraid," Jesus called to them. "It's me."

Peter, the impulsive one, said, "Hey, Lord, can I come out, too?"

"Come on," Jesus said.

So Peter threw his coat off and said "Get the camcorder rollin', guys, I'm goin' out."

Okay, okay, he didn't have a camcorder either. But do you suppose Peter's heart rate was normal as he stepped over the side of the boat?

I'm sure that some of you are reaching for your Bibles right now to search for the words *binoculars* and *camcorder.* Don't bother—they aren't there. I'm just trying to make a point, and my point is this: We often treat the Bible's stories as if they were made up, as if they didn't ever really happen to real flesh-and-blood people with emotions and fears and racing hearts. But the Bible's stories are true, and they happened to people just like us.

Just imagine if Jesus walked on the water today. Cameras would be clicking like crazy. He'd be invited to appear on Nightline and 60 Minutes. And I can just see the headlines in the skeptical press the next day: JESUS CAN'T SWIM!

Try this. When you read the Bible, use your imagination to get into the lives and minds and emotions of the people in the stories. Imagine that it's *you* that these things are happening to.

The Bible is a living book. Jesus is a living God. Let them come alive for you.

VERSE OF THE DAY:

For we do not have a high priest who is unable to sympathize with our weaknesses, but we have one who has been tempted in every way just as we are—yet was without sin.   —Hebrews 4:15

HEY!

That verse tells us that Jesus felt and experienced the same things we do. Remember that, as you read the story of Jesus walking on the water in Matthew 14:22-36.

JUST DO IT:

Now that you've read about Jesus walking on the water in Matthew 14:22-36, put the story into your own words—and try to imagine how *you* would have felt if you were Peter, every step of the way.

A SURE-FIRE WITNESSING TOOL

"Are you tired of your friends laughing in your face when you try to share the message of Christ's love?" asked the speaker enthusiastically.

"Yes!" the group of teenagers shouted back.

"Would you like to have a communication tool that will make your friends *want* to listen?"

"Yes!" they yelled.

"Well, I've discovered a method that works every time," he said. He opened his briefcase and took out a .357 Magnum. "Don't leave home without it."

When the laughter died, he said, "You know, many times our insensitive approach to witnessing is about as offensive as holding a gun to the person we're trying to share with. No wonder our friends are turned off."

I listened to that speaker's presentation with great interest. Witnessing is one of the toughest things we do as Christians—and there seems to be no middle ground. We're either too "hot" and corner people against their will to preach hellfire and brimstone and try to push them down onto their knees to pray the sinner's prayer right on the spot, or we're too "cold" and never witness at all. Which are you?

Mind if I offer a few tips that will help both the "hot" and the "cold"?

1. *Invite, don't demand.* Give your friends the *opportunity* to hear about Christ from you. If they decline, that's their privilege. Don't corner them and make them listen whether they like it or not. God gives them a choice, and so should we.

2. *Respect your listener.* Don't regard your friends as merely "targets." These are people for whom Christ died. Give them a chance to respond and listen carefully when they do. When you speak, speak respectfully.

3. *Give some thought to what you're going to say.* It's impossible to predict exactly how a witnessing conversation is going to go, but you should at least be prepared with the basics. Think through your own testimony and know how to present it in only a couple of minutes; know which Bible verses to use to illustrate the main points of the salvation message; memorize a good, simple, point-by-point presentation of the Gospel. That way you're respecting your friend's time by not having to fumble around for what to say.

4. *Earn the right to be heard.* If you haven't lived like a Christian, if you haven't been a good and trustworthy friend, then your witnessing may do more harm than good. Earn the right to be heard by living a life your friends will admire. Earn the right to be heard by being honest about your weaknesses. Earn the right to be heard by living compassionately and uprightly.

Do those things, and you won't need a .357 Magnum.

VERSE OF THE DAY:

Always be prepared to give an answer to everyone who asks you to give the reason for the hope that you have. But do this with gentleness and respect. — 1 Peter 3:15

HEY!

Want to know where in the Bible we're told to witness to our friends about Christ? Read Matthew 28:19-20 and Acts 1:1-8.

JUST DO IT:

What better way to learn these principles than to practice them? But don't bite off more than you can chew. Trying to save the whole world—or even just all of your friends—would be overwhelming.

So ask God to give you the opportunity to witness to just one person. Review the four principles one more time and be prepared to use them when God opens the door.

MAY I HAVE A LONGER LEASH, PLEASE?

DAVE

I was sitting in an airport one day, reading the paper and waiting for my flight, when something bumped against my leg and I looked up to see what it was. A little boy, a toddler about two years old with lots of energy, was careening off everything in sight, grabbing and touching everything he could reach—but his reach was restricted by his mother, who literally had him on a leash attached to a harness around his chest.

That's horrible—she treats him like a little dog, I thought. *It would be so much better just to hold his hand.*

I felt differently a few months later when I was walking out on a pier over the ocean. The water was rough—waves were crashing against the pilings; spray was flying high in the air. And I saw another mother who also had her young son on a leash. Like the boy in the airport, this boy was straining in all directions, pulling against her control.

I realized two things about that leash. First, it actually gave the boy more freedom. His mother could have picked him up and carried him to keep him from falling off the pier, but he'd have been unable to explore, to use his muscles, to touch and experience for himself.

And second, that leash was saving his life. Without it, he'd have been over the edge of that pier in a second. He'd have fallen twenty yards or so into a sea so rough that no lifeguard could have saved him.

He wasn't trying to kill himself. He was just too young to understand the dangers. So his mother exercised some control over him in a way that may have bothered some of those who saw it but that saved the boy's life.

No big deal, really. Parents routinely save their kids' lives. They don't usually do it with a leash—they do it by saying *no*.

"No! Don't stick that nail file into that electrical outlet."

"No! Don't eat that rat poison."

"*No!* Stay away from that busy street."

As we get older, our parents are still trying to save our lives and our happiness, even though we wish they wouldn't. And they do it with the same two-letter word.

"*No!* Don't play around with drugs and alcohol. That stuff can kill you."

"*No!* Don't hang around with that crowd. They're not good for you; they'll get you into trouble."

"*No!* I don't want you so much as *kissing* your boyfriend, much less getting sexually involved!"

Do your parents sometimes try to control you in ways they don't need to? Probably. But remember: They *did* save your life with that dreaded two-letter word plenty of times, and they know it. And maybe, just maybe, they're right at least part of the time.

Talk to them about it. Let them know where you feel you can handle more freedom. But leave them the right to say no.

It saved your life before.

And it may again.

VER/E OF THE DAY:

My son, keep your father's commands
and do not forsake your mother's teaching.
Bind them upon your heart forever;
fasten them around your neck.
When you walk, they will guide you;
when you sleep, they will watch over you;
when you awake, they will speak to you.
For these commands are a lamp,
this teaching is a light,
and the corrections of discipline
are the way to life.

—Proverbs 6:20-23

HEY!

Want to know what you'll get for obeying and honoring your parents? Read Exodus 20:12.

JUST DO IT:

Most kids would like to have total freedom to do whatever they want whenever they want. Since that's unrealistic, maybe you can identify some areas—bedtime, curfew, telephone use, decisions about music or clothes—where you think you can now exercise more freedom responsibly than your parents are allowing you. Think through your reasons ahead of time and then ask your parents to set a time when you can talk about it.

But don't do that unless you're prepared to accept a no without getting angry and arguing. That would hurt your case rather than help it.

MR. WILSON TAKES HIS DAUGHTER FOR A WALK.

I was doing a comedy concert at a large church in Texas, and everything was going beautifully. The lighting was good, the sound system was great, the audience was enthusiastic, and my routines were right on the money.

In other words, it was the kind of situation custom-made for some major unforeseen disaster.

The disaster hit about halfway through my show when a man who had been laughing uncontrollably had a heart attack. Several minutes later, they lifted him onto the gurney and hurriedly wheeled him out.

That sort of interruption has a tendency to put a damper on comedy. My first guilty thought was that perhaps I was to blame. It had happened right after one of my funniest routines, while the audience was laughing hysterically. I decided to write him a letter of apology.

His return letter was better than any other positive reviews and accolades I've ever received. It went something like this:

Ken:

I don't worry about dying. I prepared to meet my Lord many years ago. And please don't apologize. I've had four heart attacks. I want to thank you for the best heart attack I ever had. I'll recover to laugh again. Keep bringing Christ's joy to others.

Now there's a man who knows the *real* source of joy and laughter. Not Ken Davis's comedy routines but the Christ whose love for us, whose death on the cross, whose resurrection makes our joy and laughter possible.

And that's why it's okay for Christians to laugh and cut up and be goofy and grin. Who has better reason?

Take advantage of that freedom. Learn to laugh uproariously. Learn to appreciate a good joke. Learn to treasure the light moments of life.

It's your privilege as a Christian.

OKAY, YOU CAN LAUGH NOW

VERSE OF THE DAY:

A cheerful heart is good medicine. — *Proverbs 17:22*

HEY!

Joy is one of the fruits of the Spirit; want to find out what the rest of them are? Read Galatians 5:19-25. Compare the two lists in those verses—which sounds better to you?

JUST DO IT:

Today, examine two things:

First, make sure you've committed your life to the Christ who came to deal with—and overcome—the most serious issues of life.

Second, knowing that you are secure in him, lighten up! Look around you. You may, for the first time, see a reason for joy.

Lighten up and laugh again!

Maybe it's just because I have two daughters, but I can't understand why we can never get ready for church on time. When I'm ready and they're not, I go to see if I can hurry them up. And I find them playing with their hair.

LET ME HEAR YOUR BODY TALK

They pull it down, and then they push it back up. And then they spray it, and then they wash it out. Then they pull it down, and then they push it back up. Then they pin it, and then they unpin it. Then ...

And it goes on and on. And hey, I'm not just picking on the girls. You guys do the same thing, except it's a shorter process, and when you get done you look at yourselves and say, "Here I come! Lucky world!"

Why do we do that? Because we *care* about our bodies—about how they look, and about how they feel. And the parts of the body care about each other.

We wake up in the night, and our throats say, "I'm thirsty. Get out of bed."

And the whole rest of your body says, "No!" But the throat says again, "I'm thirsty—I'm not going to let you sleep! Get out of bed."

Then your stomach grumbles, "Hey—listen to your throat. Get out of bed." So you get up—and your toe says, "Turn on the light." But your throat says, "No—because I'm too thirsty to waste time!"

And when you smack that toe against the door frame, the throat says, "Okay, I agree—turn on the light!"

See? We spend a lot of time making sure that our bodies are well taken care of. Unfortunately, we also make some choices that hurt our bodies. It's a funny thing—yes, we want our bodies to look and feel good, but we often don't eat as well as we should, and we sometimes put into our bodies things that we know can hurt them.

Does God care? Of course. God loves us, and because he does, he cares what we do to our bodies. In fact, today's verse might surprise you, because God cares a great deal more about your body than you think he does.

VERSE OF THE DAY:

Don't you know that you yourselves are God's temple and that God's Spirit lives in you? If anyone destroys God's temple, God will destroy him; for God's temple is sacred, and you are that temple.   —*1 Corinthians 3:16, 17*

HEY!

Here are a couple more verses that say it in a little different way: 1 Corinthians 6:19, 20.

THINK ABOUT IT:

A couple of questions for you: Are you doing anything to destroy God's temple, your body? What can you do to keep his temple holy and healthy?

*O*ne of the most frustrating and heartbreaking problems for those of us who work with young people is that every year, every month, even every day, so many teenagers take their own lives.

IS DYING COOL?

Because it's such a serious and common problem, we want Jumper Fables to address it, but neither Ken nor Dave feel qualified to speak about the feelings that might lead someone to take his or her own life. So we'll let a young lady named Sarai, who has had some firsthand experience with suicide attempts, speak for us.

Even if suicide is the furthest thought from your mind, please read this anyway. Someday you may feel differently. Or today someone you love may say, "I just don't want to live anymore."

It was two years ago. I was in my room; my mom was in her room watching TV. Nobody else was home.

I was sitting in front of my mirror with a glass of water and a bottle of pills. Why did my life always have to be so screwed up? Why did God hate me so much? My friends had said they'd always be here for me. Sure. Tonight I was depressed and I needed to talk to someone, but they were all out—just because it was a Friday night. I was grounded. I took a couple of pills and then looked at myself again. I took a few more and sat back and looked at my life.

It didn't look like much. I had spent most of my life alone since I was a little girl. I had moved from place to place too often. I had been in and out of mental hospitals, had been on medication of one kind or another for it seemed like forever, and once a psychiatrist had told me that I was hopeless. I had been rejected ever since I could remember, and now even my friends weren't here for me. Alone. Again.

Why did God always desert me when I needed him most? I felt like everybody had this evil plot against me. I was so lonely, like I was the only one on my side in this battle of life, like nobody else was as screwed up as I was. I felt so depressed I didn't even want to move. I just cried.

I took a couple more pills and thought about my choices. I could finish off this bottle of pills. Then I'd be rid of all my problems and wouldn't have to worry whether or not they got mad at me or my deals went through. Or I could just face my mom and tell her that I took a bunch of pills and that I thought I needed to go back and get some more help.

That thought made me wanna laugh. Me? Tell her that I needed help and that I'd done something wrong? No way. I'd get grounded forever.

I finished taking the pills and then lay down to go to sleep. I snuggled up with my wuzzle and thought about what I had just done. Was it really what I wanted? Of course. It was the most painless way to do it. I felt sick to my stomach, but I tried not to throw up because then it wouldn't work right.

But I threw up that night anyway before the pills had finished their job. They had almost finished it, though, and I was taken to the hospital. A few days later, I went back to the mental hospital.

That was only two years ago. All the hurt and pain that I felt that night I took the pills seem like something from another life—and at the same time, it's still very real. Now I'm nine months sober; I'm a recovering drug addict and alcoholic. If I had died that night, I wouldn't be alive now to enjoy my sobriety.

It's been a long, hard trip to get from where I was to where I am. But it was worth it. Life is hard for everybody—and harder for some than others. Some get more benefits than others: brains, good looks, money. But material things aren't as important as having yourself—and having life. It's never hopeless; you can change things.

It's true that sometimes, even now, life really seems hopeless, and I just want to give up. But it's all in the way I look at it. Things won't happen for me unless I make them happen. But even if somebody has only five minutes to live, that's five minutes he or she could change. It's never too late, it's never too soon, and it's definitely never too hopeless.

Sure, you may be thinking. *That's really uncool. What will people think if I deal with my depression? If I get counseling, they'll think I'm a nerd.*

But is dying, just because I don't stick up for myself, cool?

VERSE OF THE DAY:

*The Lord is close to the brokenhearted
and saves those who are crushed in spirit.* —Psalm 34:18

HEY!

*For a complete look at how much God cares and what he offers to help the bro-
kenhearted and the "crushed in spirit," read the rest of Psalm 34.*

JUST DO IT:

Depression and suicidal thoughts are nothing to ignore. If you've
felt the way Sarai felt, get help. If you don't think you can talk to your
parents, talk to your counselor at school, or youth pastor, or pastor, or
teacher, or some adult friend.

Sarai's making it. And so can you.

If you're not one of those who sometimes considers taking your
own life, then spend some time today praying for those at your school
and church who do. Reach out in kindness to everyone you meet; your
actions and words can be a ray of hope to someone who feels hopeless.

BURNING YOUR PRIORITIES

Years ago, when I was a teenager, I sat in a youth meeting and listened to a speaker talk about identifying the important aspects of our lives.

"Don't waste your time working toward goals that aren't really important to you," he said. "Figure out what really *is* important to you, what really matters, what you really want to accomplish—and then work toward that."

He gave us five pieces of paper and had us write on each of them one of the top five aspects of our lives. Relationships, abilities, goals, talents, dreams—anything that was a top priority in our lives at that time went onto those sheets.

Choosing those five priorities wasn't easy. Lots of things popped into my mind, and it was hard to choose the top five. It was like writing a Christmas list that can only have five things on it—you feel bad about all the things you're leaving off! I did plenty of erasing and rewriting.

Then he made it even harder. There was a fireplace in the room, and he pointed to it and said, "Okay—now you have to narrow your list to four. Take one of the pieces of paper and throw it into the fire."

Wow—was it ever tough to choose which one to burn! But when we'd done that, he pointed to the fire again and said, "Now narrow it to three."

You know what's coming, don't you? He made us narrow our priorities down to one—the thing we wanted above everything else. Today, I don't remember any other details of the man's speech, and I can't even remember his name—but after all these years I still remember what I had written on that last slip of paper!

And I'm glad I had to do that, as hard as it was. Because he was right. Those who succeed in life succeed because they know what they want and are willing to bypass some other things that might be pleasurable in order to accomplish the one thing they value above all else.

Do you know what you would write on your five slips of paper? Do you know which slip of paper you'd keep at the end? And do you know how God and his will for your life fit into those plans? I'm glad someone made me answer those questions early in life.

VERSE OF THE DAY:

Seek first his kingdom and his righteousness, and all these things will be given to you as well.
— *Matthew 6:33*

HEY!

Let's see how important the apostle Paul considered his relationship with God to be in comparison with everything else: Read Philippians 3:7-9 and 12-15.

JUST DO IT:

It's never too early to set the right course for your life, and no priority is greater than the one Paul chose in Philippians 3:8: "I consider everything a loss compared to the surpassing greatness of knowing Christ Jesus my Lord, for whose sake I have lost all things." Once that priority is in place, all of the other goals in your life should contribute to it.

With that in mind, conduct your own little priority-setting exercise, just like the one I described above. And when you're done, you should be able to answer this question: *What is the overriding purpose of my life?* Then ask yourself another question: *How will I commit the daily goals of my life to the Lord?*

This is a very important exercise. You might want to discuss it with a parent, youth worker, or trusted adult friend.

"I ONLY FORGOT ONE THING."

A friend of mine left home one night with explicit instructions for his eighteen-year-old daughter. She was responsible for her younger sister, and under no circumstances was she to leave her alone.

But after the parents left, friends invited the older girl out, and she couldn't resist. "You need to promise me," she told her little sister. "First, don't tell! Second, lock the doors behind me. And third, don't leave the house. Promise?"

"I promise," the younger girl replied, eager to please her sister.

Then the older girl drove off with her friends, leaving her sister alone with plenty of pizza. She planned to be back in time to clean up any incriminating evidence. She covered all the bases except one: She forgot to take the keys to the house.

When she returned, her little sister had fallen asleep. The sleeping girl didn't hear the doorbell; she didn't hear her sister pounding on the doors and windows. The neighbors, however, were not asleep. They did hear the ruckus, and they called the police, thinking that a burglar was trying to get in.

When the parents came home, red lights from police cars were flashing everywhere, but those flashing lights were no redder than the very red face of their very embarrassed daughter.

If you had seen that girl at school the next day and asked her what went wrong, she might have grumbled something like, "God must be on my parents' side." He is, actually, but that's only part of the story. He's on her side, too. And yours.

Doesn't it seem sometimes as if God sent some little tattletale guardian angel to spy on you and tell your parents what's going on?

Haven't you and your friends often gotten in trouble when you thought you had things planned out just right—only to discover that you'd "only forgotten one thing"? I've lost track of the times parents whose kids were sneaking out in the middle of the night have told me that they discovered that deception because they woke up in the wee hours and for some mysterious reason just felt they needed to get up and check on everybody.

My point is this: If you're planning to deceive and disobey your parents, there is no perfect plan—because a God who loves you and who gave your parents responsibility for you could stack the deck in their favor at any time. For your sake, more than for theirs.

Right now, that may sound to you like a dirty trick. But that's looking at things backward. The dirty trick was disobeying and lying to your parents in the first place. God hates deception.

And because he hates deception, you should know before you try to deceive your parents that the likely results are not good.

Maybe they'll find out, and you'll get in big trouble, and your parents' trust in you will be destroyed.

Or maybe they won't find out. Maybe you'll think that since you got away with it once, you can get away with it again, and you'll begin a pattern of deception that'll last your whole life.

And that will be far worse.

VERSE OF THE DAY:

Whoever of you loves life
and desires to see many good days,
keep your tongue from evil
and your lips from speaking lies.
Turn from evil and do good;
seek peace and pursue it.

—Psalm 34:12-14

HEY!

Want to know what kind of person God really chooses to bless? Read Psalm 32:2.

JUST DO IT:

Sad to say, we live in a society where lying and deceiving come naturally. That bothers me so much that one day I made a commitment to live by total truth for the whole day. *It'll be a snap!* I thought. *I'm such an ethical person I won't have any problem.*

Right. I was amazed at the number of times that day I was tempted to twist the truth just a little. But I'm glad I tried that experiment. Now I'm much more aware of how easy it is to let the tongue speak lies, without even really thinking about it.

Try this: Since you're a much more ethical person than I am, make a commitment to be totally truthful for one week. Believe me, God will quickly begin to show you some areas in your life that need work. And when he does, remember today's verse: "Turn from evil and do good."

When I was a kid, I usually sat right next to my cousin Jim in my Sunday school class. One Sunday our teacher was discussing a Bible verse one phrase at a time and then asking members of the class to tell what they thought the phrase meant. The members of the class were merely parroting back to the teacher the kind of answers she wanted to hear. Even at that age, I knew that their answers didn't make much sense.

One boy, for instance, was asked to explain the phrase: "and the disciples left the house." Dutifully, the boy thought for a moment and then in a quavering, religious voice, immortalized this bit of wisdom: "The four walls to the house represent four kinds of sin—the lust of the eyes, the lust of the flesh, the lust of money—" Here he paused.

I could see that he was running out of lusts.

There were four walls; if this interpretation was going to be any good, he had to come up with one more lust. "—and the lust of lying," he continued. "When they walked out of the house, they escaped from the clutches of those lusts and from the evil of Satan, represented by the roof."

I could see his self-delight with that last bit of divine improvisation. And the teacher praised him enthusiastically for his understanding of Scripture.

My cousin was bent almost double trying to keep from bursting out in laughter. Seeing him about ready to explode, the teacher scowled, "Perhaps you have a better interpretation, Jim."

Jim's face became sober, but I could still see a smile tugging at the corners of his mouth. Adopting the proper quavering voice, he said, "This is a verse that has touched my soul. When the Scripture [he even rolled the first "r" in Scripture the way some preachers do] says the disciples left the house, I believe that God is trying to tell us—" Here he paused, looking heavenward. "He's trying to tell us that the disciples left the house."

When the laughter died down and Jim had been properly dealt with for his smart-aleck answer, the class continued.

But Jim had been right. It didn't take a degree in Greek to know that the words were simply communicating that the disciples had left the house. Looking back now, I regret that the kids in my Sunday school class were learning that the Bible was to be manipulated to say what we want it to say. Even at that age, many of us resented that approach and were growing to resent and mock Scripture as well.

The Bible is God's Word. It has many depths of meaning, but it should not be molded and manipulated to say what we want it to say, or to fit our preconceived ideas. When you read the Bible, read it with the expectation that God's Spirit will direct you through his Word. God can change lives, and one of the ways he chooses to do that is through the Bible—but God can change our lives only when we listen to what he truly has to say.

Don't put words in God's mouth. Let him say to you just what he wants to say—no more, no less.

VERSE OF THE DAY:

All Scripture is God-breathed and is useful for teaching, rebuking, correcting, and training in righteousness, so that the man of God may be thoroughly equipped for every good work.   *—2 Timothy 3:16*

HEY!

Want to know some of the other great things God's Word accomplishes in our lives? Read Psalm 19:7-11. (This is really good! Read it!)

JUST DO IT:

Have you ever kept a Bible-reading journal? It doesn't have to be anything fancy or time-consuming. Just get a little notebook, or even a few sheets of paper stapled together. Then, each time you read anything out of the Bible, write down the date in one column, the passage of Scripture in another, what you learned from it in a third column, and then leave a fourth column blank. In that fourth column, you'll record the ways you apply that Scripture.

Try it—you'll find that it really helps you to remember what you've learned.

*S*hortly after I graduated from college, I was starving and desperately in need of money. Then I heard about the possibility of selling home study courses; there was a $150 commission on the sale of each course! That was a small fortune at the time.

There was just one small problem: I didn't think the course itself was very good, and I couldn't imagine how it would really do much to help the customer. But the money was more than I could resist. I signed on to sell the course.

WHAT ARE YOU SELLING?

It took me seven days to perfect what I thought was the most dynamic sales presentation ever devised. My presentation was so fantastic that I was tempted to buy a study course for myself! The day my presentation was perfected, I sold the first course. The next day I sold two. My customers were so eager to buy, I couldn't believe it. After selling five courses, feeling rich with $750 stretching my pockets, I decided it was time to try to sell one outside my family. I had run out of relatives!

After just two days of turndowns and slammed doors, I quit. Had I been selling a product I believed in and felt would really help my customers, I might have had the motivation to weather those rough times. But money was my only motive. At the first sign of resistance, I gave up.

The best sales people in the world are those who really believe in their product.

I once bought enough Girl Scout cookies to feed a country just because the little salesgirl was so excited about the product. I knew it wasn't just a canned sales talk because she was eating cookies the whole time she gave it.

Listen to guys talking about their first car: "Man, it'll go zero to sixty in three seconds! It's got four on the floor, nine hundred horses under the hood, and a quadruple bypass double-overcam ram-jet carb with—" And on and on and on. It's so obvious: They love that car!

Listen to a girl talking about her boyfriend: "He's got these really beautiful blue-tinted contact lenses, see, and like these really big, really ripply muscles? And he's just so-o-o-o-o handsome! And he—" She can talk about him for hours. With great enthusiasm.

Neither of those people need an excuse to talk about what they believe in.

Maybe one of the reasons we find it hard to witness is that we're not sold on the product. We haven't really examined the depths of God's love; we haven't really considered what he has saved us from. It's one thing to witness just because your youth leader said it's the thing to do. It's another thing to be so sold on Jesus that it's hard to keep quiet.

VERSE OF THE DAY:

That is why I am so eager to preach the gospel also to you who are at Rome. I am not ashamed of the gospel, because it is the power of God for the salvation of everyone who believes: first for the Jew, then for the Gentile. —Romans 1:15, 16

HEY!

The guy who wrote the verse of the day spent much of his life in prison for what he believed. He was eventually killed because he wouldn't keep quiet about Jesus Christ. Read Romans 8:38, 39 to see just how much he believed in the power of Christ's love.

THINK ABOUT IT:

Are you really sold on the message of God's love? When we understand the sacrifice Jesus made on our behalf, and the difference God's power can make in our life, then our witness becomes more than just the fulfillment of our Christian responsibility.

If you really believe what he has done for you, you'll find it hard to keep quiet.

O n the farm where I grew up, we had a sheep named Herman. I was crawling under a fence one day when Herman came running from a hundred yards away and butted into me. He butted me right into the fence. It was a barbed-wire fence—an electric barbed-wire fence. I was carrying a couple of buckets of water.

I invented slam dancing that day.

Herman hit me three or four times while I was jerking around on that fence with electricity shooting through my body.

I made a vow while I was still impaled on that electric fence: *I'm gonna get this sheep.*

A couple of days later, standing by the barn, I looked around the corner and saw Herman coming. This was it! I looked around for something to hit him with. There was nothing.

Just the barn. I couldn't lift it. I tried.

Herman stuck his head around the corner just then, and I had nothing to hit him with. So I just yelled: "Boo!"

He died.

He looked up, and I could see it in his eyes. *That's it,* he seemed to say. And he died.

But then I had to tell my father.

My father said, "What happened to Herman?"

"Well, Dad—he came around the corner of the barn, and I went 'boo'—and he died."

How do you explain something like this?

"Now, Son, you hit that sheep."

"No, Dad, I went 'boo' and he died. Killed him. Honest! I just went 'boo.' "

I don't know whether my dad ever believed me or not. But I learned one thing that day for sure. Sheep die easy.

Unlike you and me, right? We're tough!

Wrong. We die easy, just like sheep.

Some of you are lucky to be sitting here reading this book today, just as I'm lucky to be sitting here writing it. The difference between your being here and not being here is inches. Pressure on a steering wheel that can't even be measured. A degree or two of difference in temperature that can create ice on a street corner.

We think we're invulnerable. We think we can live forever. Teenagers, especially, think they can live forever.

And, in a way, of course, we can. God has made it possible for us to live forever. But not in these bodies. If the ice on the corner doesn't get us, we'll still grow old and feeble and eventually die.

Sheep or people, it's all the same. We die easy.

What a morbid thought, right? Not necessarily. Once you realize that God has created this really great place for the people who turn their lives over to him—a place with "many mansions"—then the reminders in the Bible that we're going to die are a little like when your parents take you to the fair or the park and call out to you just as you're about to head out with your friends, "Remember—we have to leave at six o'clock." They're just reminding you to make the most of your time because it will soon come to an end and it will be time to go home.

God, too, is reminding us to make the most of our time before we go Home.

Someone once wrote:

"Only one life—'twill soon be past;
Only what's done for Christ will last."

How are you using your time?

VERSE OF THE DAY:

Remember your Creator
in the days of your youth,
before the days of trouble come
and the years approach when you will say,
"I find no pleasure in them."

—*Ecclesiastes 12:1*

HEY!

Just because death is a reality doesn't mean we have to be afraid of it. Read Hebrews 9:27 and 28, and see what Christ has done that takes away the sting of death.

JUST DO IT:

Someone once said that we should live as if today were the last day of our life. There are undoubtedly many things you would want to do on that last day, several things you'd like to say to the people you love, and steps you'd like to take to get to know God better. Make a list of those messages and steps. Why not communicate those messages and take those steps now—today! Come up with a plan.

JUMP!

My two-and-a-half-year-old daughter stood at the very edge of the stairs, seven feet above the hardwood floor, looking down as though she might really jump.

"What are you doing?" I shouted. She seemed a bit young to be thinking of ending it all.

"Just looking," she answered. "It's scary when I look over the edge. It makes my rear feel funny."

When I stopped laughing, I had an idea. This was a good chance to help her get over her fear and also to test how much she trusted me. I stood below where she was teetering on the edge. "Jump!" I said. "I'll catch you."

She inched toward the edge, took a deep breath—and then scrambled back to safety. She did the same thing several more times as she tried to work up the courage to jump. Each time I reassured her that I would never let her fall, and each time she would lean out a little bit further before cringing back. Finally, with a desperate groan, she leaned out so far that she could not turn back. With arms flailing and a scream tearing from her throat, she fell—and I caught her just as I had promised.

Suddenly she realized she was safe. A smile wiped all fear from her face, and she yelled, "Let's do it again!"

This is the same kind of trust that God wants us to have in him. He doesn't expect us to scream, "Go for it!" as we leap blindly into thin air. He just wants us to lean on him until we can't turn back. And that can be scary.

Someone once asked, "How much faith does it take to swim across a swimming pool?" A little boy answered, "Just enough to let go of the edge."

Many times we listen to those tense feelings in our rear more than we do the promises of God.

What are the edges you cling to that keep you from discovering that God can be trusted?

A boyfriend or girlfriend?

A car?

A group of friends?

A party life-style?

Don't expect to feel brave as you let go of some of your handholds of security and trust God. At first you may kick and scream just as my daughter did. God doesn't promise that following him will be painless or easy, but he does promise to be there to catch you when you need him.

VERSE OF THE DAY:

Trust in the Lord with all your heart
and lean not on your own understanding;
in all your ways acknowledge him,
and he will make your paths straight. —*Proverbs 3:5, 6*

HEY!

The Bible includes a great story about a guy who had a hard time trusting in God. In the end, this guy won his battle in a bizarre way by doing what God told him (even though it didn't seem to make much sense). Read the story of Gideon in Judges chapters 6 and 7.

JUST DO IT:

Is God asking you to do something that seems a little scary—maybe even terrifying? Is he asking you to avoid the negative influence of a particular group of friends, or to give up a habit of some kind? Maybe he's nudging you toward a career or school choice that makes you uneasy. Pray for God's guidance; talk to your parents and some adult Christian friends about it. Then, if you're confident about what he wants you to do—jump! Instead of screaming in terror, you may soon be shouting, "Let's do that again!"

THE MOST BORING SPEAKER IN THE WORLD

I've heard some long-winded speakers in my time, but the world's record for the most wind has to go the apostle Paul. Paul was so long-winded that one of his listeners died waiting for Paul to get finished.

Paul was speaking in a city called Troas. (Don't ask *me* how to pronounce it.) He met with a bunch of Christians for a meal in a third-floor room. (The Bible doesn't say which meal—could have been breakfast!) He started speaking during the meal and kept on talking until midnight!

The room was so crowded that one young man, named Eutychus, couldn't find a place to sit, so he sat on the windowsill.

You know what's coming next, don't you? Teenager on windowsill. Third floor. Speaker talks all day and well into the night.

That's right. Eutychus fell asleep. And fell out the window. And landed three floors below.

Dead.

Not funny. Except that everybody, including Paul, ran down the stairs to see how Eutychus was. When Paul saw that the boy was dead, he threw his arms around him and told everyone, "Don't be alarmed!"

Oh, sure! I don't know about you, but if I saw a teenager fall out of a third-story window and die, I'd be alarmed all over the place, and no long-winded preacher would be able to talk me out of it.

But then something wonderful happened. Eutychus came back to life. Maybe you're thinking, *He was just knocked out.* But the Bible says he was dead and that after Paul embraced him he came back to life, and they all went back upstairs and ate some more! (At least that ended the sermon.)

Of course, it was God who brought Eutychus back to life, not Paul. But here's the point: Paul was a long-winded, sometimes boring preacher; he even admitted it in 1 Corinthians 2:1. Even so, God used him to jump-start the church through his preaching and writing, and because he wrote much of the New Testament, we still read and study his sermons and writings today.

It reminds me of a husband and wife from a small farming community I was once asked to train to be youth workers. *They'll never make it,* I thought. Oh, they were wonderful people, with a strong faith in Christ and a real desire to be used, but they didn't have *flash.* They weren't *cool.* And that's what I thought it took to be a good youth worker.

Boy, was I wrong. Those two will never be great speakers. But I've met dozens upon dozens of teenagers whose lives were changed forever by the love and the example of that husband and wife.

It isn't the *size* of the gift God has given us. It's how willing we are to let him use us to do his will.

Even if you're the most boring speaker in the world.

VERSE OF THE DAY:

Not many of you were wise by human standards; not many were influential; not many were of noble birth. But God chose the foolish things of the world to shame the wise; God chose the weak things of the world to shame the strong.
—1 Corinthians 1:26, 27

HEY!

Here's a great short passage on God's ability to make strength out of our weaknesses: 2 Corinthians 12:9-10.

JUST DO IT:

Where do you think you are weak? What are you frightened of in your walk with God? Getting up in front of people to tell what God has done for you? Talking with friends about becoming Christians? Talking about your faith with your family? Trusting God to handle things you can't handle on your own? These verses tell us that we need to learn to trust God when we're in over our heads, and he'll be faithful in turning our weaknesses into strengths.

How can you remind yourself to trust him next time you're in one of your "weak" situations? List the steps you'll take. (Hint: Memorizing some of the verses listed above might be a good starting point.)

TELLING EDDIE TO GET LOST

DAVE

It was the fall I went into eighth grade. Just my luck: I got transferred that year to the junior high that was the rival of the school I'd gone to in seventh grade. I knew I was going to have it tough.

But I made a few friends and by November I was doing okay—until Eddie showed up, walking across the grass one morning looking lost, his eyes lighting up when he saw me like he'd found a long-lost brother.

Eddie had gone to the same school I had attended the year before. He was a pale, unco-ordinated, timid, slow kind of a guy. I didn't really like him, but he'd tagged along with me some the year before, and I hadn't stopped him.

But this was different. This was eighth grade, a different school, and I was fighting for my life, socially speaking. I had a hunch that Eddie was going to make it harder.

I was right. Three days later, he found me at lunch. My friends and I always sat on the grass by the girls' gym to eat out of our brown bags, and suddenly there was Eddie, sitting down beside me. "Hi," he whispered.

"Uh—hi," I said, as my new friends suspiciously eyed this awkward newcomer whose clothes and clumsiness spelled g-e-e-k.

Later one of my friends asked, "Who's the jerk?"

"What jerk?"

"You know what jerk."

"Just a guy I knew last year. Ignore him."

"Gladly—as long as he doesn't eat lunch with us anymore."

But eat lunch with us he did—all that week and the next. In fact, it was clear to all of us that he intended to make a habit of it.

The last thing I wanted was for him to hang around. He endangered my hard-won standing with my friends. But that same insecurity made me sensitive to Eddie's feelings. I didn't want him around, and I didn't want to tell him to get lost.

When I sat down to lunch the next day with my half-dozen

friends, one of them said, "Where's your pal?"

"He's not my pal. Maybe he's eating lunch somewhere else."

"He'll be here. We want you to tell him to bug off. We don't like him hanging around."

And who should appear at just that moment, walking across the grass as if he were afraid the people he passed were about to throw rocks at him.

"Here he comes," one of my friends whispered. "Just tell him to eat lunch somewhere else." We all went silent as Eddie sat down. And the silence lasted a long time after that. Nobody was going to say anything until I got rid of him. So I looked at him for the first time since he'd sat down, and the first thing that popped into my mind was what Jesus had said: *Blessed are the merciful, for they will be shown mercy.* Eddie smiled his timid little smile.

"How're you doing?" I asked.

"Fine."

I took a bite of my tuna sandwich. Was it worth it? There was no way to do this nicely. *Blessed are the poor in spirit, for theirs is the kingdom of heaven.*

"How do you like this school?" I asked.

"It's okay."

"You, uh—made any friends?"

"Yeah—you guys." One of my friends choked on his Twinkie.

"I mean, any other friends?" Another friend glanced up at me and nodded.

"Uh—I guess so," Eddie said. By this time, he had no doubt where I was heading. He'd been through it before. His smile was still there, kind of frozen, but his eyes showed how he felt. I figured I'd better move in for the kill.

"Don't you ever eat lunch with any of them?"

He shook his head.

"You really ought to."

He looked down and fingered his celery. All my friends sat quietly eating, looking at their lunches.

"Why don't you go eat with them right now," I said. And I wasn't asking. *Whatever you did for one of the least of these brothers of mine, you did for me.*

Eddie got up then, still smiling, hesitating a little as if he thought I might laugh and say, "It was just a joke, Eddie. Come on back and sit down here by me." But I didn't. And Eddie turned away and walked across the grass, carrying his brown bag.

I don't remember ever seeing Eddie again after that. He probably ran whenever he saw me coming. But if I ever do see him again, we have a score to settle. For one thing, Eddie owes me a kick in the pants. For another, I owe him a thank-you for all the meanness his pain has saved me from.

Since that day, I've met a lot of people I could have stepped on to get what I wanted. But in each of those faces, as I stand deciding, I see Eddie's last-chance eyes, waiting for the axe—and that little voice echoes: *Whatever you did for one of the least of these ...*

VERSE OF THE DAY:

Be kind and compassionate to one another, forgiving each other, just as in Christ God forgave you. —*Ephesians 4:32*

HEY!

How we treat those who are less fortunate than we are isn't just a joke; it's serious business. Here's a really important passage about it: Matthew 25:34-46.

JUST DO IT:

We don't like to admit it, but we all have Eddies in our lives—people we have treated poorly, often because we think they will hurt our social standing. Who are your Eddies? Think of one or two people you should have accepted but didn't. What can you do to make their lives easier today? Think of something specific and then follow through.

I grew up believing that if you didn't smoke, drink, go to the theater, play cards, dance, or run around with people who did those things, you were a good Christian.

One day as I sat on the porch, Ralph, my collie dog, walked by. Suddenly it hit me. Ralph didn't smoke, drink, go to the theater, dance, or play cards! And we never let Ralph run around with dogs who did.

Ralph, by the logic I was using, was a better Christian than I was! The best Christians in the universe must be the mannequins you see in department stores—they don't do anything.

Obviously, there must be a flaw in that argument. Later, I realized the truth: Being a Christian has nothing to do with a set of rules. Instead, it's an inside-and-out change of heart that comes from experiencing the personal forgiveness of Jesus Christ. That knowledge changed my perspective. Instead of reacting to the temptations of life by saying, *I can't do that because there's a rule against it,* I could now honestly say, *I don't want to do that because of the values I believe in.*

Do you see the difference? Anyone can memorize a set of rules. But if all you have is a set of rules, then you obey them for one reason only: to stay out of trouble. As soon as you realize you can break some of those rules and not get into any trouble (at least not immediately), there's no reason not to break them. If, on the other hand, your desire is to respond to God's love by living in ways that please him, you'll make your decisions in accord with those values even when there are no rules.

We begin to gain those values when we turn our lives over to Jesus Christ, and his Holy Spirit comes to live within us.

What freedom! To be good not because we have to but because we want to. Ralph was just a dog. He couldn't live that way, regardless of how many cigarettes he didn't smoke, or how many bad dogs he avoided. But we can.

Are you?

RALPH, THE DOG, WHO KNOWS THE LORD

VERSE OF THE DAY:

Therfore, if anyone is in Christ, he is a new creation; the old has gone, the new has come!
—2 Corinthians 5:17

HEY!

Have you ever taken that first step of asking Jesus Christ to come into your life? If not, read John 3:16-21.

JUST DO IT:

Think over these questions:

Do you live your life in response to the rules others have set for you? Or have you allowed God's love to motivate you to love him in return by living according to the guidelines he's given us in the Bible? First John 4:19 says, "We love because he first loved us." Reflecting on what God has done for you, how do you want to demonstrate your love for him in your life?

A man was hiking through a mountainous area one day when he came to the top of a high, rocky cliff from which he could see for many miles. It was a clear day, and he stood at the edge of the cliff for a while, resting from his hike and enjoying the view. Suddenly, the loose ground at the edge of the cliff gave way beneath his feet, and he plummeted over the edge!

Fortunately, he was able to grab a branch of a small, scrubby tree growing out of the side of the cliff as he fell. But when he looked up, he realized that there was no way for him to climb back up.

He knew he couldn't hang that way for long. He needed help. And even though he'd seen no one else at the top, he yelled, "Help! Somebody help me, please!"

Imagine his surprise when a deep, echoing voice answered from high above him, "I will help you."

But when the man looked up, he saw no one. "Where are you?" he shouted.

The voice came back, "I am God, and I will help you."

"Throw me down a rope!" the man yelled.

"I don't have a rope," God replied.

"If you don't have a rope, how can you help me?" the man cried in frustration.

"Do you trust me?" God asked in his booming voice. *What choice do I have?* the man thought, but he called back, "Yes, I trust you!"

"Do you *really* trust me?" God asked again.

"Yes, I really trust you—but please hurry, I'm losing my grip!"

"If you really trust me," God said, "let go of the branch."

The man was silent for a moment, and then he yelled out, "Is there anybody *else* up there?"

A funny story. We laugh at the audacity of the man who would dare, when God tells him what to do, to try to find another way.

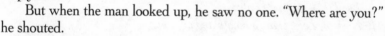

117

But guess what. We do the same thing, time after time.

God tells us how to find the greatest happiness in our families: husband and wife staying together, children respecting and obeying their parents. But we distort his plan, because we think we can find more happiness another way. And we hurt ourselves immensely by doing so.

God tells us how to enjoy the greatest sexual happiness: Wait until marriage. But we decide that we know what's best for us, and we don't wait. And once again, we hurt ourselves.

God tells us to avoid drunkenness. We think we know better, so we turn to alcohol and drugs. And destroy ourselves.

God offers to save us—not with a rope, but with the shed blood of his Son, Jesus Christ. And we turn away to save ourselves through our friends, our careers, our pursuit of pleasures—through our own efforts.

And each time we turn away from God's offered help, we're as foolish as that man hanging from the branch. God's advice may not have sounded the wisest to him as he hung there, but it was better than anything he could have come up with on his own.

VERSE OF THE DAY:

Surely God is my salvation;
I will trust and not be afraid.
The Lord, the Lord, is my strength and my song;
he has become my salvation.

—Isaiah 12:2

HEY!

Want to know how much David the Psalmist trusted God? Read Psalm 18:1-3.

JUST DO IT:

Only you know the areas of your life where he wants you to let go of your own securities and let him take over. Trust him with one of those areas today. Let go!

*S*everal years ago, I met a man unlike anyone I had ever met before. His name was Mike O'Hara. He was in his early twenties, and he was dying from bone cancer. But that's not what made Mike so unusual. It was his attitude toward life and death that amazed me.

NINETY DAYS TO LIVE

His sense of humor was astounding. Shortly after he lost all his hair from chemotherapy treatments, for instance, Mike went to a costume party dressed as a can of roll-on deodorant.

Despite his sense of humor, I was always uncomfortable around Mike because I couldn't get it out of my mind that he had only a few months to live. One day as we sat eating in a restaurant, Mike noticed my uneasiness.

"What's the matter—do you think this is contagious?" he asked, pointing at his bald, shiny head.

When I didn't answer, he laughed, rubbed his hands on his head, and then leaned forward suddenly and rubbed them all over me. "It *is* contagious!" he roared. He had the whole restaurant looking at us.

"I know why you're so uptight," he continued, more calmly. "It's because I'm dying, isn't it?"

His image blurred as the tears filled my eyes, and I nodded, too overcome to speak.

Then Mike said something that I will never forget. He leaned forward and whispered, "Ken, we are both dying. The only difference between me and you is that God has let me know *when* I'm going to die. We could step out of this restaurant and you could get hit by a Volkswagen Beetle and beat me to heaven.

"Don't be afraid of dying, Ken. We're Christians. We have nothing to lose."

VERSE OF THE DAY:
For to me, to live is Christ and to die is gain.   —*Philippians 1:21*

119

HEY!

Matthew 6:19, 20 tells you one of the reasons Mike really knew what he was doing. Read it—and then continue reading Mike's story below.

THINK ABOUT IT:

Not long after we met, Mike died. But not really. He took his last breath on this earth—and when he took his next one, he was with Jesus.

One of the reasons we often neglect the important things in life is that we trick ourselves into thinking that life will never end. Why worry about the tough stuff now? There's always tomorrow.

No one likes to think about his or her life ending. Especially my teenage friends. But if what God has said is true, then life is a wonderful opportunity to do things that will make an eternal difference.

If you knew that you had only a limited time to live, how would you live differently from the way you are living right now? What relationships would you cultivate? To whom would you apologize? Where would you spend your time and energy in the short time you had left?

Mike was right. Each of us is limited in the time we have to live. And none of us knows exactly how long that time is. Today would be a good day to start making the changes you described above. It's not too late.

My most embarrassing moment? I've had so many I have a hard time choosing, but here's one that has to rank near the top.

Picture a church roller-skating party—and there I am, at fourteen, about two lengths behind my current heartthrob. Feeling uncharacteristically dashing (I'm wearing a sweater without any moth holes in it), I put on a little speed and reach out to touch her arm, intending to skate up beside her. (Oh, unspeakable boldness!) "Hi," I say.

She turns her head slowly, gives me a funny little smile, I melt into those beautiful brown eyes—and then I find myself skidding on my nose across the painted concrete floor and coming to rest as a pretzel. Our skates had touched, and, full of gracefulness, I had stumbled.

ON THE SKIDDING RINK FLOOR

DAVE

Through my shoelaces, I see her laughing over her shoulder at me as she skates gracefully away.

Terry, a college-age guy I know, glides past just then with his arm around the beautiful girl he's engaged to. "*Aha!*" he chuckles, winking at me. "Saw the whole thing, you sly devil."

What? That's it? That doesn't sound like such a big deal. Why was that so embarrassing?

It wasn't—not to Terry and his fiancee, who, after all, had other things on their minds and undoubtedly forgot all about my little embarrassment within fifteen seconds. And not to Kathy, the girl I was after, who may have chuckled at my expense for all of an hour or two.

But to me, it was a nightmare. I had made a move toward the girl I loved and had proven myself a fool in front of the whole world. And even before I sprang to my feet, red-eared, and skated on as if nothing had happened, the question had exploded in my mind, *Did she do that on purpose? Sure she did—and everybody knows it!*

I couldn't sleep that night. I played the scene over and over in my head, and each time it got worse. My face was hot, constantly, for days.

I had trouble keeping my mind on anything. I did poorly in my classes. I couldn't bring myself to talk to Kathy, or even to look at her.

Too much of my ego got splattered over the concrete floor in that fall. Since I already had doubts about my gracefulness and my appeal to girls, that rebuff (accidental or intentional—I never did ask her whether she did it on purpose) and clumsy fall were all it took to convince me that I was a washout, all around.

It was at least a month before I finally decided that everyone else had either forgotten about it or hadn't noticed it in the first place, and that people weren't laughing at me behind my back.

All that over something so minor? Why did it matter so much, and why do I remember it so vividly years later? Because one of the most universal and troublesome characteristics of the teenage years is low self-esteem. In all likelihood, you too have experienced what I just described—some minor mistake, or some off-hand remark that seemed so horrible that you spent hours, days, maybe even weeks depressed and unhappy.

You'll survive that low self-esteem. It will probably even do you some good, although that's a little hard to believe when you're sitting alone in your room, depressed, bored, angry, and abandoned.

Remember these things: You aren't the only one. It won't last forever. And there are ways to lessen the pain and make your life more pleasant right now.

I wish I could have remembered, as I skidded across that skating rink and heard people laugh, that I am a child of the King, with no need to be ashamed.

VERSE OF THE DAY:

For we are God's workmanship, created in Christ Jesus to do good works, which God prepared in advance for us to do.   —*Ephesians 2:10*

HEY!

Want to find out just how carefully God created you to do those good works? Read Psalm 139:13-16.

JUST DO IT:

"For we are God's workmanship," today's verse says. Remember what Genesis 1 says about God's workmanship? "And God saw that it was good." What's good about the way God created you? There are definitely many good things, so make a list. And if your list is short, that's because you aren't aware of what the good things are yet. So pray that God will show you the side of yourself you aren't seeing yet—the side that God created for all those good works he has in mind for you.

LEARNING THE LANGUAGE

My daughter Taryn flew into the room in a new outfit. "How do you like my dress?" she asked.

One of the things I have learned in my more than forty years of life is that *that* question, especially coming from a wife or a daughter, is a loaded one, almost impossible to answer correctly on the first try. On this particular day, my first answer was a dud.

"It's fine," I answered, meaning that it met my standards for decency, was functional, and looked good.

"You hate it!" she pouted. In her mind, "fine" is what you say to someone when you've taken the conversation—and the relationship—about as far as you want to take it. As in, "Fine! Have it your way!"

To communicate to her that I really *liked* the dress, I had to use language that *she* understood as complimentary. "That's a rad dress, Taryn, and it makes you look, like, totally beautiful."

Okay, don't barf. So more-than-forty-year-olds aren't all that great at teenage slang. At least my heart was in the right place, and Taryn gave me credit for it. "Thank you!" she said, and ran from the room beaming.

Believe me, this is no attempt to say that teenagers can't understand plain English. All of us, of all ages, demand the same language clarification, because the same sentence too often means two different things to two different people. If I want to tell my wife she has a face that makes time stand still, but instead I say, "Honey, you've got a face that would stop a clock," I'm in trouble, no matter how good my intentions.

God certainly understands this truth. He knows that if he tried to speak to us out of a huge thundercloud, with lightning flashing in all directions, in a deep voice booming "I LOVE YOU!" we'd never understand. We wouldn't feel loved; we'd feel frightened. So instead, he chose to send his son Jesus to come down and live among us and speak plainly about God's love for us and his plans for us, backing up every word he said with the demonstration of his life.

The apostle Paul preached and lived the same way, as his words in today's verse show.

What does all of that have to do with you? Not much—unless you want to reach your friends and your family with the message of God's love. In that case, you'll need to learn their language.

VERSE OF THE DAY:

I have become all things to all men so that by all possible means I might save some.
                                                                    —1 Corinthians 9:22

HEY!

The story of Paul preaching in the Greek city of Athens is a great example of trying to "speak the language" of the people you're trying to reach. Read that story in Acts 17:16-34. In what ways is he tailoring his message for the ears of those around him?

JUST DO IT:

If you wanted to reach a foreign tribe with the Good News of Christ, you'd have to learn their language and culture and then communicate with them in ways they understand.

As you try to share God's love with your friends and family, these suggestions may help you to speak that good news in *their* language:

1. Listen carefully to them when they're talking.
2. Ask questions to make sure you're understanding what they're saying and to show interest.
3. Try to use language that isn't "churchy."
4. Make sure that you back up everything you say with your life. Otherwise, your words won't count for much.

THE TOUGHEST QUESTION

What's the toughest question facing Christians today? I think it's the same question Christians have been asking since Adam and Eve walked in the Garden.

I can't tell you how often both teenagers and adults have said, "Ken, I've got a tough decision to make, and I don't know how to decide because I don't really know what God's will is for my life. I've tried and tried to figure out what he wants me to do with my life, and I still don't know."

Until you and I know what God's will is for us, how do we decide about things like marriage? And jobs? What classes should you take next semester? What about relationships? Where should you go to college?

I sometimes wonder whether Satan himself isn't involved in some of this confusion about God's will. He couldn't have found a better technique for paralyzing us! As long as we're confused about what God wants of us, we can't make decisions. Then we get angry toward God, because we feel like he's way up there in the cosmos somewhere, looking down on us, snickering, saying, "I have a perfect will for you. And you don't know what it is! Na na na na na!"

Fortunately, that isn't the kind of God we have. We can know God's will. Paul tells us how in Romans 12:1 and 2:

> Therefore, I urge you, brothers, in view of God's mercy, to offer your bodies as living sacrifices, holy and pleasing to God—this is your spiritual act of worship. Do not conform any longer to the pattern of this world, but be transformed by the renewing of your mind. Then you will be able to test and approve what God's will is—his good, pleasing, and perfect will.

In those two verses, Paul lays it out almost like a formula. I can know God's will for my life if I:

(1) Give God my body as a living sacrifice,
(2) Give God my will by letting him control my life, and
(3) Give God my mind by keeping it pure and flooding it with his Word.

126

Do those three things, Paul says in Romans 12:1 and 2, and we can prove what God's will is—his good, pleasing, and perfect will.

This idea is so important that we'll devote the next four daily readings to it. And we hope it helps. After all—what's more important than knowing God's will?

VERSE OF THE DAY:

The world and its desires pass away, but the man who does the will of God lives forever.   *—1 John 2:17*

HEY!

It's a good idea to prepare yourself for your search for God's will over the next few days by reading the rest of Romans 12—start with verses 1 and 2, which we quoted above, and then continue through the end of the chapter. Great stuff!

JUST DO IT:

What are the real questions you have about finding God's will? Long-range questions, like career or marriage partner? Day-to-day things, like how to wear your hair, or whether to pierce your ear? In preparation for the next few days, list the major questions you have. I'm not saying you'll have the answer to all of those questions by the end of the week, but you'll have some critical insights that will help you see those questions in a new light.

GOD WANTS YOUR BODY

The first step in finding God's will, according to Romans 12:1: Offer your bodies to God as living sacrifices.

Imagine this conversation: A young man walks proudly out of a youth rally and says, "I gave my life to God."

"That's good! But what did you give him?"

"My life."

"But what *is* your life?"

Pause. "You know." Another pause. "My *life*."

"*Life*" is a nice, general term. Too general, in fact. When you turn your life over to God, what changes? What does it mean?

Let's get specific.

Your life is wrapped up in a package that you understand very clearly, and that package is your body. As long as you think in general terms, like "life," it's easy to forget that the things we do with our bodies day by day might not be pleasing to God and might not be appropriate for someone who's given his "life" to God.

The apostle Paul didn't mess around with misconceptions. In a letter to the Christians in Rome, he got right to the point: "I urge you, brothers,…to offer your bodies…to God." Your *bodies*.

Little kids understand this very well, because they haven't learned to generalize yet. So they come home from Sunday school singing,

"Be careful, little hands, what you do.
"Be careful, little hands, what you do.
"For the Father up above is looking down in love,
"So be careful, little hands, what you do."

And then they keep on going:

"Oh, be careful, little eyes, what you see.
"Oh, be careful, little feet, where you go.
"Oh, be careful, little ears, what you hear."

Hey, we could have a whole anatomy lesson based on that song! They might not let us sing it in Sunday school if we did, but after we're about twelve years old we wouldn't sing it anyway. We're too cool.

Instead, we'd rather think in general terms about giving our "lives" to God because then we don't have to think about what these hands do, and what these eyes see, and what these ears hear.

Are you truly committed to Christ? Do you want to experience something that will transform your Christianity? Today, walk around singing that kids' song:

"Oh, be careful—"

Don't sing it out loud, or somebody will come and take you away. But if you sing it to yourself, you'll become aware of something that has always been true: God is aware every moment of what we're doing with our eyes, our hands, our feet, and with all the parts of the body— not so that we'll feel guilty, but because he wants to use each of those parts of our body to affect people's lives for eternity.

How will you use the parts of your body today?

VERSE OF THE DAY:

Do not offer the parts of your body to sin, as instruments of wickedness, but rather offer yourselves to God, as those who have been brought from death to life; and offer the parts of your body to him as instruments of righteousness.
—Romans 6:13

HEY!

Read these verses, and find out what God thinks about your body: 1 Corinthians 3:16-17.

JUST DO IT:

Pick just a couple of body parts—eyes, maybe, or hands, or ears, or feet. (Or *anything*. It's your body, so you don't have to be embarrassed about which part you choose.) Be conscious as you go through the day of how you might use or treat those parts differently if you consider them to be individually consecrated to God.

And if this exercise isn't a real surprise and challenge—then you're not paying attention!

Tomorrow we'll continue examining Paul's instructions for finding God's will.

LIVING SACRIFICES

It just doesn't make sense, does it? *Living sacrifices.* It's like "jumbo shrimp." Or "pretty ugly." Words that just don't go together.

"Good grief."

"Mobile home."

"Educational television."

"Military intelligence."

I mean, think about it. There weren't many sheep that came back from the sacrifices. What would they say? "I was at the sacrifice last night. They chose me. Oh, I'm feeling a little burnt out, but other than that—"

But when Paul urges us in Romans 12:2 to present our bodies as *living sacrifices* to God, that's exactly what he means. God doesn't want a dead sacrifice. Dead sacrifices don't please him anymore because he already sent his Son to pay for our sins. What he wants is our living bodies, dedicated to him. Living sacrifices.

Living sacrifices are scary, because if they want to, they can crawl right off the altar! God doesn't strap people to the altar, saying, "Here's what you're going to do, and you're going to do it right now!" A living sacrifice determines in her own mind and heart that she will stay on the altar, dedicated to the Lord. Every part of her being belongs to God because that's where she *wants* to be. Or—she determines to cop out and leave. Because she's a *living* sacrifice, the choice is hers.

And when a living sacrifice is given the opportunity to sin, he doesn't say, "I can't—it's against my religion." He says, "No, I don't choose to live that way. And the reason I don't choose to live that way is that I belong to God."

That's the beginning of knowing God's will. If we are truly living sacrifices, then God's will and our own will are the same. God's will becomes more than some unwelcome set of rules or instructions imposed on us by God, some roadmap to life we'll grumble about at every turn. If we are living sacrifices, the choices God wants us to make will be the choices we'll want to make, for reasons of our own. We'll make those choices of our own free will.

Living sacrifices.

Are you there yet? Neither am I. But we'll get more help over the next couple of days as we continue this examination of Romans 12:1, 2.

VERSE OF THE DAY:

For it is God who works in you to will and to act according to his good purpose.
—Philippians 2:13

HEY!

Read Romans 6:4. According to that verse, Christ's resurrection has made it possible for us to be living sacrifices, instead of dead ones!

THINK ABOUT IT:

In what ways does your Christianity go beyond a dead, legalistic set of rules? How can you take part in the new life made possible by Christ's death and resurrection so that you remain a sacrifice but shine as a *living* sacrifice?

DON'T LET THE WORLD PRESS YOU INTO ITS MOLD

"Do not conform any longer to the pattern of this world," Paul says in Romans 12:2. Or, to put it another way: Don't let the world press you into its mold. And that's the second step in knowing and proving what God's will is: determining your purpose. To me, determining my purpose means following Christ. It means going God's way rather than my way.

For many years, my ministry was mostly a way for me to get affirmation from people. And because my motives were weak, my commitment to personal integrity was also weak. I lived one kind of life when I was with the people I was ministering to, and I lived another kind of life when I was somewhere else. I have determined in the past several years that I have one purpose: to be what God wants me to be.

"Sure," you may be saying, "that's easy for you to say because you have a very glamorous life-style."

You can believe this or not, but if tomorrow God called me to a mission field where there was nothing—no applause, no accolades, no money, no laughter—I'm ready to go. My family has discussed that possibility many times, and someday you may see that decision lived out if God chooses to call us that way.

My purpose is not to entertain, nor is it even to become a great preacher. My purpose is to serve a living God, any way he wants me to serve him. My purpose is to follow Christ. I want my life to reflect that from morning till night. To someone who conforms to the world's patterns—earn lots of money, try to get ahead, look out for yourself and who cares what happens to others—that purpose must look pretty stupid. But I don't care, because when I made the decision to live for God, I stopped trying to impress the world.

Here are some words that should disappear from your vocabulary forever: "What will my friends think?" I meet teenagers every week who've never accepted Jesus Christ as their Savior and Lord because they're afraid of what their friends will think. I meet teenagers who have already trusted Christ as their personal Savior but who continue to live as if Jesus Christ doesn't even exist. And to all of those teenagers, Paul's message is not, "You rotten slimeballs—how could you be so weak?" Paul simply says, "Don't let the world press you into its mold. Determine that your purpose is to follow Christ, and then don't be moved."

The second step in knowing God's will for your life is to determine your purpose. And your purpose should be to not let the world press you into its mold but rather to follow Christ.

VERSE OF THE DAY:

Blessed is the man
 who does not walk in the counsel of the wicked
or stand in the way of sinners
 or sit in the seat of mockers.
But his delight is in the law of the Lord,
 and on his law he meditates day and night.
He is like a tree planted by streams of water,
 which yields its fruit in season
and whose leaf does not wither.
 Whatever he does prospers.   —*Psalm 1:1-3*

HEY!
Another great passage that says the same thing in a different way is 1 Peter 1:14 and 15.

THINK ABOUT IT:

What is the purpose of your life? Can you identify one? And if you can, how consistent are your actions and decisions with your stated purpose? Are there areas of your behavior that conform more to the pressures of this world than they do to your purpose?

Ask God to help you change that pattern.

PURIFY YOUR MIND

"Be transformed by the renewing of your mind," Paul instructs us in Romans 12:2. That's the third step in knowing what God's will is for us. We've looked at the first two in the past couple of days. First, we give God our bodies; second, we determine our purpose. Now the third step—we purify our minds.

And that, Paul says, is a step so radical that we will be literally transformed.

How is this radical step accomplished? The answer is found in Psalm 1, verses 1 and 2:

> Blessed is the man
>> who does not walk in the counsel of the wicked
> or stand in the way of sinners
>> or sit in the seat of mockers.
> But his delight is in the law of the Lord,
>> and on his law he meditates day and night.

In other words, we purify our mind by avoiding the things that could pollute it and meditating on the things that help make it pure.

First, we have the responsibility to guard our minds against the kinds of garbage that threaten our purity. When what we're watching or hearing isn't what God wants us to watch or hear, we need to get up and turn it off—even when there's no one else in the room to know. And here's a tough one: When our friends are saying or watching things that we know pollute our mind, we need to say to them, "I'm going to leave." We need to stand up and walk out of the theater. We need to reach over and turn the dial on the radio.

I'm not writing this so that I can preach to you about sex on television, or about rock music, or about the movies. I don't think I have to. You already know that some of it is directly opposed to all that God loves. And when it is, we shouldn't need a preacher to tell us that it's not God's will for us to sit there and listen to it.

Yeah, I know it's hard to live that way. Sometimes it isn't easy to be a Christian. But don't forget that Psalm 1 also tells us what happens to those who purify their minds by putting a "garbage guard" at their mind's door and meditating on God's Word: "Whatever he does prospers."

The second part of purifying our mind is to flood our mind with the positive influence of God's Word. Every year, I gain more respect for the Bible—God's record of who he is and how he wants me to live. The Bible is what God is using to purify my mind! Oh, sure, I've got a long way to go. But this book works!

I want it to work—on me. I don't want to be just another writer. There are plenty of writers already. I don't want to be just another preacher or speaker or just another comedian. There are plenty of preachers, plenty of speakers, plenty of comedians. What do we need? We need men and women, preachers and comedians, writers and athletes, and plumbers and teenagers who are totally sold out to God. Even one person sold out to God can make a difference—think what will happen when we have hundreds and thousands! But we won't—until those men and women and teenagers decide to purify their minds so they can be transformed into the men and women and teenagers God wants them to be.

Purify your mind. It's the final step in answering the toughest question Christians face: finding God's will for their lives.

VERSE OF THE DAY:

How can a young man keep his way pure?
By living according to your word.
I seek you with all my heart;
do not let me stray from your commands.
I have hidden your word in my heart
that I might not sin against you. —Psalm 119:9-11

HEY!

Today's verses were from the 119th Psalm, which is all about the Word of God. Read the whole thing—it'll help you understand just how important the Bible really is! Yeah, I know it's long. But it's worth it!

JUST DO IT:

Today, notice the kinds of things you allow to flood your mind: things you choose to think about out, or allow yourself to watch or hear. You might be surprised at how much you've learned to tolerate that clearly dishonors God! Decide on some limits for yourself and decide how you're going to enforce those limits. (There *are* ways to control your thought life; people who say it's impossible just don't want to.) Guard your mind!

Then, take a few minutes to evaluate the importance of God's Word in your life, based on how much time you spend with it. If you're too much of a stranger to the Bible, pick some ways to change that. Consider how often you read the Bible, how much you know about it, what use you make of what you read.

This is important; don't just blow it off!

IS IT A BEAR OR IS IT MEMOREX?

t's night. You're walking down a path in the woods. It's spooky. There isn't much moonlight; you can't see well at all; and you're hearing strange noises you wish you weren't hearing. You catch a glimpse of something moving through the trees ahead of you—something big—and suddenly a huge black dog walks across the path.

At this point, your whole body gets involved. Your eyeballs send a message to your brain: "It's a bear!"

And your feet don't argue with your eyeballs—your feet don't say, "I don't *think* so; let's go check it out." Your feet say, "Let's take the body to a new place."

And you burn a hole in the ground getting out of there. Why? It wasn't a bear! It was just a black dog on his way to see his girlfriend, and he didn't have time to waste on you. Friends, it doesn't matter if you're looking at a piece of cardboard, or a rock, or a shadow, or a dog, or a hamster—if you *think* it's a bear, you'll respond the same way as you would if a huge grizzly bear were right there breathing down your neck.

We may be wrong in what we think, but we will act on what we think is true anyway, just as if it *were* true. Solomon said it a little differently years ago when he wrote the book of Proverbs, but it's just as true today: "As he thinketh in his heart, so is he" (Proverbs 23:7, KJV).

You are what you think. It may be a bear, or it may be a hamster, but if you *think* it's a bear you'll run just as fast either way.

If you're brave enough, I challenge you today to examine your life—the way you act, the things you say, the things you're afraid of, the kinds of relationships you have, and how you conduct yourself within those relationships. Then conclude what your life shows that you really believe about God. Because if you believe that God is all-powerful and loving, you'll behave one way. If you believe that God is angry and vindictive and just waiting for you to screw up so he can zap you, you'll behave another way. If you believe that God is blind, or asleep, or just doesn't care, you'll behave yet another.

What does your behavior tell the world about what you believe about God?

VERSE OF THE DAY:

As he thinketh in his heart, so is he. — *Proverbs 23:7, KJV*

HEY!

Read James 2:18-22 to see how what we do demonstrates our true faith and belief.

JUST DO IT:

Today, pay attention to your own behavior. What are your friends seeing in you today? What does that tell them about your belief in God?

As a child and as a teenager, I loved to be in front of people—so much so, in fact, that I was often called a show-off, hungry for attention, selfish, egotistical. And sometimes the people who called me those things were right.

EARNING MY LIPS

So when my high-school English teacher invited me to stay after school one day, I knew it wasn't a social invitation. I had just spent the hour disrupting her class.

She stared at me in silence for about a minute. (It reminded me of the silence that precedes a tornado.) Then, quietly, she said, "Ken, I want you to go out for speech."

"Speech!" I sneered "You've got to be kidding." All my friends walked around school wearing letter jackets with macho sports symbols on them—symbols like crossed hockey sticks, footballs, and baseball bats. I wasn't going to be caught walking around with a set of speech lips hanging from my jacket. "What makes you think I can do anything in speech?" I asked.

She looked me right in the eye and said, "Ken, with a single sentence you can make everyone in this class laugh, destroying a teaching atmosphere it has taken me most of an hour to create. That takes ability. Why not use that ability in a positive way?"

She pestered me until I entered speech competition in the Humorous Interpretation category. I won almost every contest I entered. Because of her persistence and encouragement, today I travel full-time, using my gifts to entertain and help people. Most important, I use them to share around the world the wonderful message of God's love.

Okay—a nice story, but it happened a long time ago (about a million years) and you're wondering what it has to do with you. And the answer is: *God has given you abilities that are to be used for his glory. Don't waste them!*

We all have those gifts, but we don't all use them as God intended us to. Some of us don't use them at all. And just as I used the ability God gave me in communication to disrupt classes and make my teacher pull her hair out, the very things that are getting you into trouble now with your parents, your teachers, or your friends, may be the things that, when you learn to use them correctly, will one day make you an effective servant of Christ!

I've finally earned a set of lips for my letter jacket—and I'm proud of them! Who says God doesn't have a great sense of humor?

VERSE OF THE DAY:

Each one should use whatever gift he has received to serve others, faithfully administering God's grace in its various forms. —1 Peter 4:10

HEY!

If we all have different gifts, how do we know whose gifts are the top ones? See Romans 12:3-10.

JUST DO IT:

As a teenager, I had some God-given talents that weren't being put to good use. You may be making better use of your gifts—or maybe not. Today, see if you can come up with a plan to identify the strengths and talents God has given you and make better use of them. Don't be afraid to ask for someone else's help with this—especially if you don't think you *have* any gifts! (God doesn't lie, and he told us in the Bible that we *all* have gifts to use.)

Really and truly can't identify those areas you're strongest in? There's a questionnaire that might help; write to: Pathfinders Profile Group, 15491 East Mississippi Ave., Aurora, CO 80014.

*O*kay, get the picture: This guy named Jonah had tried to run from God by getting on a boat bound for a faraway place. But a storm had come up while they were at sea, and the sailors freaked out. They knew that God was more than a little upset, so they threw Jonah overboard, hoping (since it was Jonah

DO I SMELL LIKE WHALE BARF TO YOU?

that God was upset with) that God would chill out and quiet the storm.

After that, it was a good news/bad news situation. The good news was that he didn't drown. The bad news was the *reason* he didn't drown: He became a snack for a giant fish. Luckily, the fish decided not to chew, and swallowed him whole. So there he was, in the belly of the fish, and he prayed a prayer—just as you would if you ever found yourself in that situation. Here's the prayer that he prayed:

"In my distress I called to the Lord,
     and he answered me.
From the depths of the grave I called for help,
     and you listened to my cry."

Did you feel a twinge of recognition when you read those words, "From the depths of the grave"? It's sad but true that many of those who read this book will feel that they've been there. Some may have been emotionally or physically abused. Some have been involved in the kind of sin that makes you feel that you're less than worthless. Maybe some are running from God, just as Jonah was. Or maybe you have felt—or are feeling at this moment—that life just isn't worth living. You may even have been planning how you might end it. I, too, have been near all of those places. And from my own experience I want to say to you: God will hear your cry. He has not forsaken you. You are not hidden from his sight.

As you think about your own situation, do these next verses sound familiar?

"You hurled me into the deep,
    into the very heart of the seas,
    and the currents swirled about me;
all your waves and breakers
    swept over me.
I said, 'I have been banished
    from your sight.'"

Sometimes I want to cry out, "You can't see me anymore, God! Where have you gone? If there's a God, how come these things are happening?" In his own way, those are the things Jonah was saying, too. But he didn't give up hope. Instead, he said those important words God loves to hear:

"'Yet I will look again
    toward your holy temple.'
The engulfing waters threatened me,
    the deep surrounded me;
        seaweed was wrapped around my head.
To the roots of the mountains I sank down;
    the earth beneath barred me in forever.
But you brought my life up from the pit,
    O Lord my God.
When my life was ebbing away,
    I remembered you, Lord,
and my prayer rose to you,
    to your holy temple."

That was just Jonah's simple, honest cry for help. But it must have been a great prayer, because the Bible says the Lord made the fish sick so that it vomited Jonah up on the shore—Okay, I admit it, that's not the way you'd like to arrive after a cruise, but at that point I think Jonah was glad to take whatever he could get.

What's the point? The point is that there is absolutely no place on earth that Jonah—or any of the rest of us—can be separated from God so that he can't hear us and know what is happening to us. Even if it seems like he's impossibly far away. Even if it seems like your prayers go no higher than the ceiling.

God doesn't leave you when you run from him as Jonah did. God doesn't leave you no matter how bad your sin. When you have gone through difficult and painful times and have felt forsaken and alone, that doesn't mean that God wasn't there.

He is always available.

He will always hear your prayers.

Remember Jonah's words? "From the depths of the grave I called for help, and you listened to my cry."

VER?E OF THE DAY:

"Sacrifice thank offerings to God,
fulfill your vows to the Most High,
and call upon me in the day of trouble;
I will deliver you, and you will honor me."   —*Psalm 50:14, 15*

HEY!

Read what David had to say when he was hiding out from his enemies in Psalm 3. (And by the way—God delivered him from those enemies.)

JU?T DO IT:

Ever felt like you were in the depths of the grave? Or worse? Just because it doesn't *feel* like God hears you, or just because the problems you pray about don't immediately disappear, doesn't mean he's not there. From wherever you are, right this moment, why not call out to God?

God knows. He listens. He cares.

SLIDING DOWN THE GRAVEL BANK

DAVE

When I was a kid, my family used to spend our summer vacations at a cabin in the mountains. One summer—I was about four years old, I think—I wandered away from the cabin one day and down to a gravel pit I wasn't supposed to play in. But there wasn't anyone around to tell me no, so down into the pit I went. I messed around in all that neat gravel and stuff until I got tired of it—and then I discovered why I wasn't supposed to go down there.

I couldn't get out.

The steep sides of the pit were composed of nothing but sliding gravel. I could take a run at the embankment and get maybe seven or eight feet up, and then down I'd slide in a little avalanche of tiny rocks all the way to the bottom. Again and again I tried, getting more and more frightened each time, until finally I was all tears and runny nose, howling at the top of my lungs for somebody to come and get me out. You don't have a lot of cool when you're four years old.

Somebody did come. A man in faded blue jeans, big heavy boots, and a ragged flannel plaid shirt. He looked like Paul Bunyan to me, and I thought he must be a logger. More likely he was an accountant from Los Angeles on summer vacation. He gave me a hand up out of the pit, pointed me in the right direction, and sent me on my way. At four years of age, I didn't even have the good sense to be embarrassed—I was just glad to still be alive.

As I walked, something seemed very clear to me. (Even little kids have some sense.) The thing I realized was this: My problem hadn't been that I couldn't climb the bank of the pit. I could climb all right—at least seven or eight feet up. The problem was that, once I got there, I couldn't stay there—I immediately slipped right back down to the bottom. If I could have kept the seven or eight feet I'd already earned and then added another seven or eight feet, I'd have been out of there.

But I kept sliding back down.

I was like the football team that makes thirty yards in three plays—and then loses it all again in penalties and sacks. You don't score any touchdowns that way.

Or like you when you save forty bucks toward that leather jacket you've been wanting—and then blow it all on one date. And hate yourself for it.

You probably think I mentioned all this to make some kind of point. I did. What I've just been talking about is exactly what the apostle Paul's talking about in Philippians 3:16: "Only let us live up to what we have already attained." It's a simple principle, and it makes sense in whatever you do: Once you've gained ground—don't lose it.

And what is it we're working toward as Christians? Something Paul talks about in Philippians 3:15: spiritual maturity. It's a tough goal. Once you've gained part of the way, you sure don't want to lose it. Maybe, for you, part of that journey toward maturity is gaining control over your temper. You've just about got it now, right? Fine—don't lose that ground now that you've won it. If you do, you'll just have to fight for it all over again. It's just like sliding down the gravel bank.

Or maybe for you the issue is gaining control over your appetites—for food, for sex, for alcohol, for praise. Got it licked? Ask God for the power to keep it! What we've already "attained," as Paul says, we need to live up to.

So what's the best way to keep the victories you've already won? You're doing it right now—congratulations! Keep your mind fixed on the Lord you serve and on His Word, and you'll continue to grow—and to protect the ground you've gained. After all, the best way to keep what you've already attained is to attain some more!

VERSE OF THE DAY:
Only let us live up to what we have already attained.   —*Philippians 3:16*

HEY!
The verses that come before today's verse really put it into perspective: We're working toward a goal, and we'll never achieve that goal if we keep losing ground. Read about it in Philippians 3:10-15.

JUST DO IT:

Make a list of the changes you've made in your life in the past couple of years. Maybe habits you've overcome, new areas of maturity, better ways of relating to people, or good new habits—like praying or reading your Bible.

Study that list carefully. Are you losing ground in any of those areas? If so, it's time to dig in and press on.

Don't lose ground!

On a foggy evening in New York City, a woman walked from her office to her car. As usual, she walked quickly because of the many muggings and rapes that had occurred in that area of the city. Nervously, she fumbled with her wallet as she paid the parking attendant, then headed toward the far end of the dark lot where her car was parked.

She had almost reached her car when, hearing something behind her, she glanced over her shoulder and saw a young, shabby man in a wool cap loping toward her. With a gasp of fear, she began to run.

"Stop!" the man yelled, chasing her between the cars.

Another glance revealed that he was running much faster than she was and would catch her in a moment. Just then, her toe caught on a loose brick and she sprawled painfully onto the rough, wet pavement.

The man caught up to her in an instant and stood over her, panting. "Why did you run?" he asked. "You left your purse at the attendant's shack. Don't you want it back?"

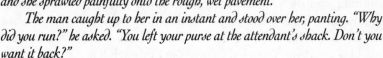

One of the most beautiful—and disturbing—poems I have ever read is a poem by Frances Thompson called "The Hound of Heaven."

In that poem, the poet flees from a God who will not cease from pursuing him:

I fled Him, down the nights and down the days;
    I fled Him, down the arches of the years;

I fled Him, down the labyrinthine ways
    Of my own mind; and in the midst of tears

I hid from Him, and under running laughter…
    From those strong Feet that followed, followed after.

After a lifetime of fleeing from God, the poet is finally caught—and discovers that God had pursued him all that time not out of anger but out of love. God wanted not to punish him, not to destroy him—but to save him.

We are so afraid that God will take from us our happiness or our security, when really that's exactly what he wants to give us.

Why run from God? Why run from the one who wants only to love you and to bring you joy?

Why are you still running?

VERSE OF THE DAY:

For God so loved the world that he gave his one and only Son, that whoever believes in him shall not perish but have eternal life. For God did not send his Son into the world to condemn the world, but to save the world through him. —John 3:16, 17

HEY!

Take the time this week to read completely through the book of John. (It's a short book—you can read through it in a week if you read three chapters a day.) The power of God's Word will help you stop running and, instead, embrace the one who loves you so much.

JUST DO IT:

Take another look at today's verse. In fact, read it out loud—substituting your own name: "For God so loved *(say your own name here)* that he gave his one and only Son, that *(if I)* believe in him *(I)* shall not perish but have eternal life. For God did not send his Son into the world to condemn *(me)*, but to save *(me)* through him.

Do you ever run from a total commitment to Christ? Why? Keeping that personalized verse in mind that you've just read out loud, write down what you're afraid will happen if you commit yourself totally to God.

Then stop running—and let him catch you up in his love.

WHAT'S THE DIFFERENCE?

DAVE

Do you like those "What's the difference between—" jokes? Like:

Wayne: What's the difference between my sister and an elephant?

Jane: I don't know.

Wayne: About ten pounds.

Or,

Fred: What's the difference between a dead gopher and a loaf of bread?

Ted: I don't know.

Fred: I'll never send you to the store for a loaf of bread.

Well, here's another one for you: What's the difference between you and an unbeliever?

You can probably come up with plenty of answers to that. But if I asked your best friends, or your brother or sister, or your teachers at school, would I get the same answers?

What *is* the difference between a Christian and a non-Christian? And how is that difference made clear? Are we supposed to speak differently? Act differently? Dress differently? Sing different songs? Not dance or drink or smoke?

When it gets down to specifics (like appropriate styles of clothes) I've got to admit that I'm sometimes not sure what's right for a Christian and what's not, but I'm sure the principle is right: There should be more than just an internal difference to being a Christian— there should be an obvious external difference as well.

Jesus said in Matthew 5:13 (New KJV), "You are the salt of the earth; but if the salt loses its flavor—it is then good for nothing."

You may be able to give a theologically accurate description of what happened inside of you when you became a Christian, but if you want to make a difference, then you have to taste different from the rest of the world. And the world doesn't use its tongue to taste you, for which I am grateful—it uses its eyes and its ears.

That's one of the reasons the fourth chapter of Philippians is one of my favorite chapters in the Bible: It talks about what distinguishes the salt from the rest of the stew.

In verses 2 and 3, he urges all of the Christians at Philippi to make peace with each other and learn to agree.

In verse 4 he doubly exhorts them to rejoice in the Lord—always! Now that's going to be an obvious difference in this world of complainers!

Verse 5 includes a wonderful bit of advice: "Let your gentleness be evident to all." Judging by our favorite TV shows and movies, gentleness isn't as highly regarded as the ability to blast holes through people who don't agree with you. But Paul points out that gentleness is definitely one of those things that makes a Christian a Christian—and our gentleness should be evident to all.

He describes another characteristic of Christians in verses 6 and 7: peace. Christians are to be known as people who don't worry about things—people who are at peace with themselves and with the world.

Then in verse 8, he tells us that Christians are people who look for the good in life and in other people—or the true, the noble, the right, the pure, the lovely, the admirable, the excellent, the praiseworthy. Stop to think for a minute about what most people you know like to hear about, and you'll realize just how radically different Paul really wants you to be.

Okay, I admit it: Paul was a dangerous man. He was utterly sold out to God ("For to me, to live is Christ and to die is gain"). He wanted no halfway Christianity—and he encouraged his readers not to settle for that either.

Let's not settle for halfway Christianity. Let's not be afraid to be obvious Christians.

VERSE OF THE DAY:

"You are the salt of the earth; but if the salt loses its flavor—it is then good for nothing." —Matthew 5:13, New KJV

HEY!

That fourth chapter of Philippians is really something—you should read the whole thing!

THINK ABOUT IT:

What makes you different from those who aren't Christians? And I'm not talking about whether or not you do the "nine nasties"; I'm talking about the real, inside-and-outside differences that make you "taste" different from the rest of the world.

Do you even *want* to be different?

If the answer is that you're willing to be different if that's what God wants you to be, then read that fourth chapter of Philippians and start working on those differences—one at a time, praying for God's help and power. A world of lost people is looking for something different. Will it be you?

DON'T SNIFF FURRY MILK CARTONS

Ever had someone say to you, "I think this milk is spoiled," and then shove the carton toward you and demand, "Smell this and see what you think"?

Crazy stuff like that happens in my family all the time. I don't know whether my wife and daughters just enjoy seeing me roll on the floor, gagging, or they just don't trust their own senses. But I do know that I've decided not to punish myself anymore. The other day my wife, Diane, held a fungus-covered milk carton under my nose and said, "Smell this!" So I followed the advice teenagers have been hearing for years now.

I just said no.

If a can of beans is bulging so badly that it looks like a metal tennis ball, I don't have to taste it to know that it's bad. If I hear someone ransacking my living room in the middle of the night and my wife nudges me and says, "Go see what that is," I don't have to see the pantyhose pulled over the guy's face to know that I've got trouble.

Call me chicken if you want, but when I sense danger I tend to move in the opposite direction.

Most of the time.

But what about those other times—times when I've been tempted by things that I knew were rotten and that could hinder my relationship with others and with God. I have seen the mold, I have sensed the danger of the temptation—but I decided to go ahead and give it a little sniff anyway.

The result of that little sniff has never been pleasant. The result of sin is death. Sin kills relationships. It destroys our walk with God. It breaks our heart and our spirit.

That's why sin is never treated lightly in the Bible. Flirting with things we know to be wrong is a fool's game, like Russian roulette. Next time you realize you're being tempted, don't sniff just to see if it's truly rotten. Instead, call on God's power to turn and go the other way.

VERSE OF THE DAY:

Submit yourselves, then, to God. Resist the devil, and he will flee from you.

—*James 4:7*

HEY!

If you find yourself wanting to smell that curdled milk, better read James 1:13-15. Remember the end result of sin—it isn't worth it, is it?

JUST DO IT:

I'm sure you've all heard of this morbid science experiment: If you put a frog in boiling water, it will hop right out. But if you put him in while the water's still cold and then slowly heat the water, you can boil the frog to death before he knows what's going on. Have you taken steps toward some action that you know is wrong? Just allowing yourself to repeatedly think about something you're tempted to do, even though you'd "never do it," is a first step. Or maybe you find yourself talking about it with your friends, or reading about it.

And before you know it, you're in hot water.

Whatever it is you're being tempted to do, reading this may be the avenue of escape God is providing. (Read 1 Corinthians 10:12, 13 right now.) Why not pray for God's power to turn from danger?

Don't waste your time sniffing those furry milk cartons. God has better things in mind for you.

"I'M RUINED!"

When my daughter Traci was just a toddler, I put her into the bathtub to take a bath one day and went to the living room to read the newspaper. Okay, okay, now I know—bad idea, very unsafe. But I was just a new parent, and I didn't know how dangerous that was. I was soon to find out.

I'd been reading the newspaper for several minutes when the sound of Traci's terrified screams coming from the bathroom panicked me. I threw the newspaper into the air and ran for the bathroom. But somehow, the door had gotten locked! As her screams continued, I started kicking the door, thinking of all the horrible things that might be happening on the other side. Had she turned on the hot water? Had she dragged an electrical appliance into the tub with herself?

I was so pumped, I actually kicked down the door! (Only took me 200 kicks.) I ran into the bathroom, little splinters of bathroom door hanging from my body—and there she was, frantically pointing to her hands. "Look!" she screamed. "I'm ruined!"

She was screaming because her hands were all wrinkled from being in the water.

When my breathing had returned to normal so that I could speak again, I spent several minutes trying to convince her that she was not going to spend the rest of her life looking like an extra-terrestrial.

"God made you that way," I said. "God made you so that, when you put your hands in water for a long time, they wrinkle up."

"Why?" she whimpered, still staring at her hands as if they might fall off any minute.

"Why?" I repeated. "Well, God told me that if you ever asked that question, I should tell you it's none of your business." Okay, I didn't know why. But I didn't want her to know that.

I know many adults and teenagers who have reacted to life much as Traci did to that bath. Some of them have committed sins they felt were so terrible that God could never love them again—like a friend of mine who committed armed robbery. Others have made bad decisions that have changed the course of their lives—like the high-school sophomore who had a baby. "I'm ruined!" they scream—and they

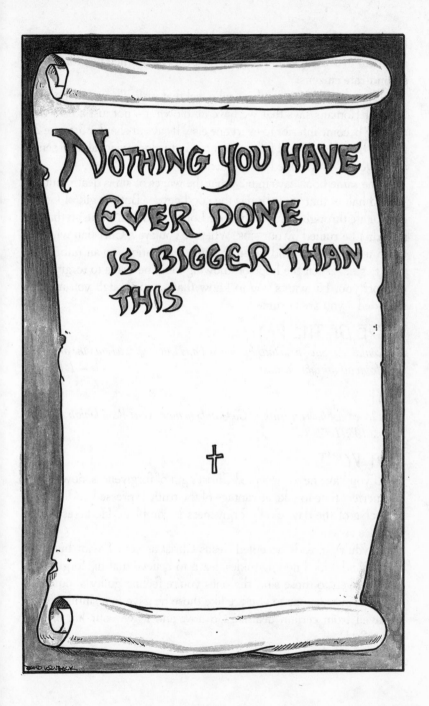

NOTHING YOU HAVE
EVER DONE
IS BIGGER THAN
THIS

✝

believe it. They believe that God can never love them again, much less use them to accomplish his will. They believe that they will forever be second-rate citizens.

I have good news for those who feel that way: There is hope! The book of Romans says that we have all blown it—not just a few, who thereby become inferior to everyone else. It says in chapter 3, verse 23, that all have sinned and fallen short of God's glorious ideal. In a sense, then, we are all wrinkled and ruined.

The same book says in 6:23 that the wages of sin is death, but the second half of that verse brings the good news: "But the gift of God is eternal life through Jesus Christ our Lord." God sent Jesus so that we wouldn't be ruined by our sins. Whether you are a Christian who has taken a wrong turn and fallen to some temptation, or an unbeliever who has never felt the hope of knowing God, he waits to forgive and comfort you. He wants you to know that, even though you may be wrinkled—you aren't ruined.

VERSE OF THE DAY:

If we confess our sins, he is faithful and just and will forgive us our sins and purify us from all unrighteousness. —1 John 1:9

HEY!

Want to see just how unwrinkled God wants to make you? Read Isaiah 1:18 and Psalms 103:11-12.

JUST DO IT:

If you have never accepted Christ's gift of forgiveness, now would be a perfect time to take advantage of the truth expressed in John 1:9, our verse of the day. God's forgiveness is complete. He takes *all* the wrinkles away.

If you've already accepted Jesus Christ as your Savior but have slipped and added new wrinkles, learn to believe that his forgiveness extends even to those sins, the ones you're feeling guilty about right now. His instructions to you are like those he gave to a sinful woman he saved from certain death: "'Go now and leave your life of sin'" (John 8:11).

This may seem at first like a sad story, but really it's one of the most inspiring and encouraging stories I know:

STANDING UP TO HITLER

DAVE

On April 8, 1945, near the end of World War II, Lutheran pastor Dietrich Bonhoeffer led a short worship service in the Gestapo prison at Flossenburg, Germany. After a short message, he was just finishing his final prayer when two guards entered and said, "Prisoner Bonhoeffer, come with us."

All of the prisoners at the service knew the meaning of those words. Bonhoeffer said his final good-byes, adding "This is the end, but for me it is the beginning of life."

The next day, April 9, 1945, Dietrich Bonhoeffer was hanged by the direct order of Heinrich Himmler, one of Hitler's generals. Why? Because Bonhoeffer, a Christian, had staunchly resisted the wicked atrocities of the Nazi regime.

The words he wrote not long before his death echo after him:

> Suffering, then, is the badge of true discipleship. The disciple is not above his master. Following Christ means ... suffering because we have to suffer. That is why Luther reckoned suffering among the marks of the true church .... Discipleship means allegiance to the suffering Christ, and it is therefore not at all surprising that Christians should be called upon to suffer. In fact, it is a joy and a token of his grace.[1]

Doesn't make being a Christian sound like much fun, does it? Suffering is a mark of the true Christian? Isn't suffering something to be avoided?

Yes—most of the time. The remarkable thing about Dietrich Bonhoeffer is not simply that he was executed—it is *why* he was executed. At a time when many—in fact, most—people in his society, even most Christians, were simply going along with what they all knew, deep down, was wrong, Bonhoeffer stood up and said, *"No!* We should not be killing Jews just because they're different from most Germans; we should not be invading other countries simply to make ourselves more powerful. Hitler is *wrong."*

He said it loudly, unashamedly, and often. He said it as a Christian should speak: in the confidence that, since the Bible told him it is right, it *is* right. And, of course, he was executed for it.

There are times when being a Christian means that you have to take the heat. There are times when the right thing to do is to stand when everyone else is sitting down, to speak out when everyone else is keeping silent, to say no when everyone else is saying yes, or yes when everyone else is saying no.

Taking that kind of stand always has a cost. Paying that cost is the kind of suffering Bonhoeffer was talking about.

When the time comes—and it may be coming sooner than you think—will you be willing?

VERSE OF THE DAY:

Blessed are you when people insult you, persecute you and falsely say all kinds of evil against you because of me. Rejoice and be glad, because great is your reward in heaven.   —*Matthew 5:11, 12*

HEY!

Want to read about some people who really suffered for their beliefs? Read Hebrews 11:32-38. And what does the Bible say about them in verse 39?

JUST DO IT:

Can you think of a time in your life when you knew the right thing to do but were afraid to do it? When you did the wrong thing (knowing it was wrong) because you were afraid of what might happen if you did the right thing? Maybe you were afraid you'd lose friends or be teased. Or maybe it was something else.

How can you find the courage, next time you're faced with that choice, to do what you know is right? (You'll find an answer to that question in Hebrews 12:1-3.)

[1] Quoted in *The Message of the Sermon on the Mount*, by John Stott (Downer's Grove, Ill. : Intervarsity Press, 1978), p. 53.

When I was asked to speak at a hayride one fall, I had serious reservations. Usually, hayrides are held outside, and there's always the possibility of distractions and interruptions. The lighting and sound system are usually poor, and the weather is invariably cold (this was in northern Minnesota). Besides that, the hayride atmosphere usually hypes kids for smooching, not worshiping. And if all of that weren't enough, on this particular hayride they would use real horses, so I'd have to watch my step.

The pastor assured me that the meeting was to be held in a barn and that he would provide a spotlight and a quality sound system. So I agreed to give the speech.

When the time came, two hundred teenagers fresh from a romantic hayride gathered on bales of hay to listen. Everything was as promised: The lighting was superb and the sound system was one of the best. The kids seemed eager to hear what I had to say. In fact, only one thing was wrong: Unknown to me, about thirty pigeons had also gathered in the barn that night on the rafters above us. I'm not sure whether they had come to hear me or whether the barn was their usual Saturday night hangout. What I am sure of is this: Pigeons are not welcome at my meetings anymore.

At intervals of about two minutes, one or another of these feathery creatures dropped a pigeon missile into the crowd. Some of these missiles hit my audience, and some didn't, but when it came to destroying my efforts at basic communication, every pigeon missile was right on target.

What do pigeon missiles have to do with your relationship with God? Just this: The way those pigeons affected that crowd of kids that night reminds me of the way our thought lives can affect our spiritual lives. They can be just as disruptive!

I know several people who feel safe because they've never actually *done* the sin but have just *thought* about it. But the potential for sin begins with the thoughts that enter our mind. If we allow that potential to grow, it can even end in death. Listen to what Jim says: "But each one is tempted when, by his own evil desire, he is dragged away and enticed. Then, after desire has conceived, it gives birth to sin; and sin, when it is full-grown, gives birth to death" (James 1:14-15).

In other words, our thoughts lead us to sin, and sin leads us to death. Yipes! That's pretty good evidence that we should be careful about what pigeons we let roost in our rafters. We can't stop them from flying through on occasion, but we do have the power to keep them from nesting there. When the pigeons of lust or anger or revenge or rebellion wing their way into our minds, we have a choice. We can take a broom and shoo them out. Or we can help them build a nest where they can grow and multiply and eventually drop pigeon missiles that can ruin our lives.

VERSE OF THE DAY:

We demolish arguments and every pretension that sets itself up against the knowledge of God, and we take captive every thought to make it obedient to Christ.
—*2 Corinthians 10:5*

HEY!

Once you get rid of those nasty pigeons, you'd better bring in the doves. "What doves?" you ask. Read Philippians 4:8, 9 and find out.

JUST DO IT:

It's amazing how much less temptation to sin we feel when we stop toying with temptation in our mind. Identify at least one pigeon you've been letting fly around in your rafters. Then bring it down and replace it with a dove. Happy hunting!

THE EX-CON
DAVE

Raised on a small ranch in Montana by alcoholic parents, Rod was arrested as a teenager when his "friends" got him to steal a car for them. There was no room in the juvenile corrections facility, so Rod, at sixteen years of age, found himself in prison.

He was there only a few weeks, but the experience branded him for life. Just as surely as if he wore a sweatshirt with the words lettered on it, he saw himself as an ex-con. And he was sure that everyone else did, too.

Mentally, Rod was slow, and his grasp of reality was dim, but in that dim light he saw a future of petty crime, alcohol, drugs, and then either a violent death or a return to prison.

Somehow, Rod wandered into a church one Sunday morning where, to his surprise, he found himself welcomed, smiled upon, and invited back. He came back a week later and was invited to dinner afterward.

Rod had found a home. This church became his family.

It wasn't easy. Rod's personal habits and his need for constant companionship often made befriending him an exercise in patience. But it reminded that little group of Christians that their weaknesses were surely as frustrating to God as Rod's were to them, and so they continued to feed him, to smile and laugh with him, to encourage him.

Despite his mental confusion, Rod heard the message they wanted him to hear: That his new happiness came from Jesus Christ.

And in his childlike heart, Rod wanted to give a gift to the one who had given him so much. He had no money; his job as a cab driver barely paid enough to enable him to live in poverty. He had no skills, no talents, no abilities.

And so he came to my door one night, since I was the song leader in that little church, and said, "I want to write a song. I want you to help me."

How can this man, who can barely speak in sentences, write a song? I wondered, but to him I said, "Sure."

So he sat on my couch and handed me a crumpled piece of lined paper torn out of a spiral notebook. There were a few lines of verse written on it. No sense of meter, no consistent rhyme scheme, lines of greatly varying length. "Well, Rod," I said, my heart sinking, "I think it needs some work yet."

"That's okay. I want it to be good. Just tell me what's wrong with it."

So I made some suggestions and sent him away, thinking, *He'll forget about it now. It's beyond him. He probably didn't even understand what I said.*

And he didn't. But he was back the next night, with the same crumpled sheet of paper, ripped now by erasures, and his new efforts weren't any better than the old ones. So I tried to explain it again. He listened again, nodding.

And the next night he was back.

It took months, but gradually his creation became recognizable as a song. There was no way that Rod, a hopeless monotone, could write the tune—or even sing it. That would be my contribution. Still, the words were his.

Finally the time came when it actually worked. The lines were all reasonably the same length, the rhymes acceptable. That was surprising enough, but even more amazing was that it *meant* something. Rod had done well. It was finished.

I will never forget Rod's face that Sunday morning I stood in front of the congregation (Rod was too nervous to sit—he was standing in the back, trembling), explained how the song came to be written, and sang Rod's song for that small group of believers. Or how he glowed after the service when they crowded around him to thank him.

Rod wasn't somehow magically transformed by this experience. Rod was still Rod—still confused and moody, still poor, still struggling with his identity.

But that doesn't negate the validity of the ministry that took place in that little church, when a lonely, angry young man—unable to function in society, at odds with the law, separated from his poor excuse for a family, found a group of people who asked nothing of him but the chance to share their Christ with him and to stand alongside him.

And because of that, Rod was able to write a song.

How many others are out there who could write a song if someone would love them enough?

VERSE OF THE DAY:

But God chose the foolish things of the world to shame the wise; God chose the weak things of the world to shame the strong. —*1 Corinthians 1:27*

HEY!

The Bible's full of stories of weak or handicapped people who succeeded in great things because God helped them. Read about Moses' lack of self-confidence and inability to speak in Exodus 3:1–4:17. He didn't think he could do what God asked him to do, but through God's power Moses led his people out of slavery.

THINK ABOUT IT:

The key words are "hidden potential." It's frustrating for anyone when they know they're capable of something but no one will give them a chance to try it. It takes a real gift to see hidden potential in someone; do you have that gift? Can you give people the benefit of the doubt and allow them to try the things no one else thinks they're capable of?

No one would have guessed that Rod could write a halfway decent song; only one person thought Helen Keller might be capable of thinking and speaking and relating to the world. But, given the chance, both of these people surprised those around them by succeeding.

Whom do you know who might have hidden potential? What can you do to help unlock that potential?

THREE BOYS IN A PRESSURE COOKER

It was the biggest rock concert in history!

The king had produced the concert in honor of himself. (He was just a little conceited.) He had even built a ninety-foot statue of himself out of gold and insisted that everyone at the concert bow down and worship him as soon as the band started to play. (Okay, he was very conceited.) In fact, he insisted that anyone who didn't bow down would be thrown into the huge furnace that sat near the statue. (Okay, he was *mega-conceited*.)

The day came. The king gave the signal. The lead guitarist, spandex from head to toe, hit a blaring chord and the rest of the band joined in the frenzied playing. The entire audience fell to their faces in worship of the golden statue. It was as if they had all been shot at once.

They all fell down, that is, except for three Jewish boys who refused to obey the king's command. The three were immediately spotted by the king's spies. (If an entire audience lies down and you choose to stay standing, you *are* going to be immediately spotted.)

The king went ballistic. He had them brought before him. "Bow down!" he demanded, "or I'll barbecue you in my furnace!"

Their response went something like this: "We don't need to argue with you to save our own skin. If you choose to throw us into that furnace, our God is big enough to save us. But even if he doesn't, we want you to know, king, that we will not serve your gods or worship your image of gold!"

The king, as you can imagine, went berserk. He had his people heat the furnace seven times hotter than usual and then ordered his baddest bouncers to tie the three boys up and throw them into the furnace. The furnace, by this time, was belching such furious flames that the bouncers were burned up as they threw the boys inside.

What the king saw next totally freaked him out. Not only were the three boys walking around in the flames unharmed, but also someone who looked like an angel had joined them. In fear and wonder, the king shouted for them to come out.

When they came strolling out of the fire, their hair wasn't singed, their clothing wasn't burned, and they didn't even smell like smoke. (There are a number of high-school students who return to class after lunch and can't claim all three of those things.) Then the king—who at least had the good sense to admit when he was beat—praised the God who had sent his angel and rescued those boys. They had trusted in God and refused to follow the king's command. They had been willing to give up their lives rather than serve or worship any god except their own God.

A couple of questions for you to think about:

1. *Do you have any gods in your life that are more important to you than your true God?*

I'm not talking about some statue hidden in your closet. I mean something like a relationship, a pattern of living, social status, or a possession.

2. *What do you think of these teenagers' faith?*

They didn't demand that God save them from the horrible death of the furnace. They believed he could, and in the strength of that faith they refused to compromise, knowing full well that he might choose *not* to save them. If you're like me, there are times when you cave in simply to avoid embarrassment.

And if you're like me, there's much you can learn from Shadrach, Meshach, and Abednego.

VERSE OF THE DAY:

Then Nebuchadnezzar said, "Praise be to the God of Shadrach, Meshach, and Abednego, who has sent his angel and rescued his servants! They trusted in him and defied the king's command and were willing to give up their lives rather than serve or worship any god except their own God." —Daniel 3:28

HEY!

Read the whole exciting story about these three brave teenagers in Daniel 3.

JUST DO IT:

Maybe this is the day to put God back in his rightful place in your life. First, if you haven't already, read Daniel 3. Then, if there are other gods you have placed before him, write their names down on a piece of paper—then burn the paper, as a symbol that you'll no longer let them stand between you and God. Ask God to give you the strength to keep him number one.

Look for an opportunity today to stand up for what you believe. Use the example of the faith of Shadrach, Meshach, and Abednego as your inspiration.

"MISSION CONTROL TO MARINER 7—"

DAVE

You're in the Mariner 7 space vehicle orbiting Mars, relaxing briefly just before you and the rest of the crew members prepare for the first manned landing—a historic moment. There's a bit of static over the communications speaker, and a voice invades your rest: "Mission Control to Mariner 7. Mission Control to Mariner 7."

"Somebody see what they want," grumbles the mission commander, strapped into his cot, resting with one arm thrown across his face.

"Listen carefully," the speaker continues. "Errors have been discovered in our original calculations. You must make several important changes in your landing procedures. Repeat: Errors have been discovered—"

"You gettin' this?" drawls another of the astronauts, sucking the equivalent of a chocolate bar out of a tube. But two of the others are asleep, and you sit engrossed in a *Reader's Digest*.

"Failure to introduce these new procedures into your mission plan could endanger the mission as well as your lives. Exact instructions follow. Repeat: Exact instructions follow. First—"

And on your capsule spins around Mars, with the specific instructions that could save your life being spoken into the air you breathe, and yet none of you is paying attention. It's a breakdown in communication of major proportions, but it isn't in the electronic equipment or in Mission Control—it's in your ears. The message is there—you just aren't listening to it.

And that, unfortunately, is a true story. Not the Mars part—at least not yet. But each of us can get our hands on the exact instructions we need to guide us through this difficult, constantly changing mission called life—specifically teenage life—and we usually prefer to sail on without them. Until suddenly there's a bumpy landing, and somebody gets hurt, and then we scramble around for our instruction booklets and scream something about, "Why does Mission Control let things like this happen?"

One of the things we've tried to do in *Jumper Fables* is encourage you to use that instructional booklet for your life—the Bible. We've tried to show, for instance, how every passage of Scripture has an important application to your life—questions you need to answer about you. (Check out 2 Timothy 3:16.) It's easy to get into the habit of reading the Bible for other people—finding in every passage you read just what Craig needs to hear, or Belinda, or Chuck. But the Bible you hold is for you. It was written just for you. The message in it is about you—not Chuck.

As a teenager, you're just beginning a new and difficult and, frankly, dangerous mission. You don't want to make the mistake of ignoring the specific instructions given for you by the One who planned the mission—and knows how it will end.

Our prayer for you is the same prayer that Paul prayed for the church at Philippi in today's verse. But getting to where that verse says we ought to be headed isn't easy. In fact, without your instruction manual, you won't get there at all.

When all else fails, read the instructions.

VERSE OF THE DAY:

And this is my prayer: that your love may abound more and more in knowledge and depth of insight, so that you may be able to discern what is best and may be pure and blameless until the day of Christ, filled with the fruit of righteousness that comes through Jesus Christ—to the glory and praise of God.

—Philippians 1:9-11

HEY!

Have you read 2 Timothy 3:16 yet, like I suggested above? If not, read it now. It'll tell you where the Bible comes from and what it's good for.

JUST DO IT:

If you're using *Jumper Fables* once a day, or even a few times a week, then you're reading at least several verses a week of the Bible. This week, whenever you're reading the Bible, make a special attempt to do two things:

1. Find in each passage you read the specific instructions God is giving you for excelling in this mission called life and respond appropriately and obediently.

2. Resist the temptation to see instead the meaning of those verses for somebody else. This week, read the Bible for *yourself*—not your brother, not your parents, not your friend. Let God show *you* what *you* need to change.

SILENCE ISN'T GOLDEN—IT'S DEADLY

I'm going to include the following story just as it appeared in my book *How to Live with Your Parents Without Losing Your Mind*, because I don't think I can say it any better than I did there.

It was 1985. I was flying in cold gray clouds at seven thousand feet, and I knew I was in trouble. An inch of deadly ice protruded from the leading edge of the airplane's wings. Icing like that had killed many pilots in the past, but I thought I could deal with it—so I began to climb.

Suddenly I smelled smoke. Within seconds, the white, acrid smoke from burning wire filled the cockpit and stung my eyes. Now the situation was critical. There's nothing more dangerous for a pilot than an in-flight fire. When it's combined with airframe icing in instrument conditions, the odds against survival are great.

Wasting no time, I radioed for help and received an immediate response. The controllers on the ground knew that my situation was grave. Because of the fire, I'd had to shut off the electrical instruments I desperately needed to fly in the clouds. I was flying blind in an airplane that was quickly turning into a popsicle. I had only one hope for survival: my link of communication with the controllers. I had to keep them apprised of my situation, and they had to keep me informed as to where I might land. Most of the airports within easy distance were closed because of the weather. Minneapolis had the nearest airport with the radar to guide me down and the fire equipment to assist if I was unsuccessful. By the time I could reach Minneapolis, there would be no fuel left for a second try. Even though it was a life-and-death situation, I felt assured that the controllers and I could work together to find the best solution to this mess.

But that assurance was quickly shaken. In order to give me proper radar coverage, the controller asked me to change to a different radio frequency. He told me that I would be talking to people who would guide me all the way down to the runway. He encouraged me to stay calm, wished me luck, and gave me the new frequency. I quickly tuned it in and asked for help. Dead silence.

For five minutes (it seemed like five years), I called for help. Without communication, I was facing certain death. I didn't have enough gas to get to clear weather and (because of the fire) I didn't have the instrumentation I needed to land in this weather. Only communication with the controller could save my life. I switched back to the old frequency. No response.

Now I was terrified. I tried other frequencies, hoping I might run into one that would get me through. In my panic, I forgot the frequency I had originally been assigned. As I frantically twisted the dial, my earphones were suddenly filled with the sweetest sound in all the earth: someone calling the numbers of my plane. The controller carefully guided my plane through the fog to a tense but safe landing at Minneapolis International Airport. If communication had not been restored that day, chances are great that I would have become a sad statistic of what happens when people don't talk.

Hard work at communication is crucial even if you're not a pilot. In fact, in every relationship you have—your relationship with God, your relationship with your parents, and your relationship with your friends, for instance—the same truth applies.

And that truth is so important that we've used three verses for today, to talk about three different levels of communication:

VERSE OF THE DAY:

Pray continually. —1 Thessalonians 5:17

For the word of God is living and active. Sharper than any double-edged sword, it penetrates even to dividing soul and spirit, joints and marrow; it judges the thoughts and attitudes of the heart. —Hebrews 4:12

But encourage one another daily, as long as it is called Today, so that none of you may be hardened by sin's deceitfulness. —Hebrews 3:13

HEY!

Take a look at what Hebrews 10:22-26 says about keeping communication open with God and fellow Christians.

JUST DO IT:

If you read the three "verses of the day" above, then you've read about the three levels of communication we must maintain:

1. *Talking with God.* (We do this through prayer.)
2. *Listening carefully as he talks to us.* (He does this as we read his Word—the Bible—and allow it to speak to us.)
3. *Communicating with each other.* (This is the fellowship and encouragement the author of Hebrews was talking about in the third verse above.)

How often are these lines of communication open in your life? Without them, you're in the same predicament as I was in my airplane that night. Check all three of these lines of communication carefully every day, patch them when they're weak, and keep them open—at all costs.

THE BRIDGE

DAVE

We got out of the car and walked across the grass toward the creek. Other families in the park were throwing frisbees or cooking hamburgers; the sound of their laughter floated through the Michigan spring air. But my daughter and I weren't even looking at each other, much less speaking, and certainly not laughing.

"Let's go sit on that bench," I said, pointing. We crossed the creek on a wooden bridge, and Sarai stopped.

"You go on ahead," she said. "I need a smoke." She fished in her jacket pocket for a pack of cigarettes.

A few days before, of course, I'd have gone ballistic if she'd tried to smoke in front of me, but today I just walked on and sat on the bench, waving my arm every now and then to try to get the clouds of gnats out of my face.

We were there to decide what to do. Things had gotten so bad in our home that both of us knew something had to change. All of us in the family knew that Sarai was using drugs and alcohol; we'd even found some of her drugs in the house. She had run away several times, sometimes staying away as long as a week. And I knew that she was sneaking out at night and staying out till nearly daylight. She was skipping school most days. And our family life had practically disappeared in the face of all the yelling and anger as we tried to deal with this daughter who, seemingly, hated us.

But today I had realized how close our family was to simply falling apart under the pressure. Sarai had skipped school, then shown up in the early afternoon at another school where her stepmom (my wife) worked. After screaming profane, insulting things for a few minutes at her stepmom—who was in the middle of a phone call—Sarai stomped out to the car and drove away, leaving my wife in tears, surrounded by the principal and teachers who'd come running out to see what the ruckus was.

Enough was enough; I couldn't allow that kind of abuse.

As I watched Sarai standing on the bridge that afternoon, smoking her cigarette, I imagined what she must be thinking of me.

Authoritarian. Cold. Out to destroy her fun. Incapable of understanding her. Angry.

The truth is, I was a man with a broken heart. The girl standing on the bridge, smoking, was the same girl I'd first seen just a few minutes after she was born, the same girl whose diaper I'd changed over and over again, and with whom I'd walked the floor night after night to get her back to sleep. I remembered all of the things that I was sure she wasn't remembering that day: tucking her in, singing her to sleep, parent/teacher conferences, drying her tears, visiting her in the hospital when she broke her wrist, watching her peacefully sleep.

Maybe, like most parents, I had a hard time telling my teenaged daughter that I loved her. But I loved her so much that it hurt. I was horribly frightened for her; she was in the process of destroying herself, and I felt helpless to stop it because there was a canyon between us that I couldn't cross no matter how hard I tried. And I knew that I would be unable to cross that canyon until something happened: until she turned back toward me and stopped running. I had come as far as I could. Only Sarai could make it possible now for us to become close and loving again. And Sarai was still running from me just as fast as she could.

She flipped her cigarette butt into the creek and came to the bench. But our conversation that day solved nothing; we were talking to each other from miles apart. And even though I didn't see how things could get any worse, in the next few days they did.

This story doesn't have an ending. Sarai and I continue to work on our relationship, so the story continues. But it has a happy continuance; Sarai spent many months in a treatment program that helped her to conquer her destructive drug habit and to understand and deal with the self-destructive feelings that caused her to live the way she did. The relationship between us as well as between Sarai and the rest of our family is warm and loving. And far wiser than it was before.

The two people who had sat on that bench, unable to say the things they were feeling, learned to talk to each other. I am easily able now to tell Sarai how much I love her. And Sarai is able to tell me what she was thinking as she stood on the bridge smoking that cigarette that day: how lonely she was for a warm, loving relationship with me. How badly she wanted to hear me say, "I love you," and to be able to believe it. How much she wanted her daddy.

Relationships grow strained between parent and child during the teenage years. There are many hard feelings and much anger on both sides. But as the distance grows, there are few teenagers who don't long for the warmth of the relationship they've lost with Mom and Dad. And there are few if any parents who don't lie awake nights wondering how to bridge that gap so that they can take their angry child into their arms and say, "It'll be all right. I love you."

That's what your parents want. Give them what Sarai finally gave me: the chance to love their child again.

VERSE OF THE DAY:

"Honor your father and your mother, as the Lord your God has commanded you, so that you may live long and that it may go well with you in the land the Lord your God is giving you."   —*Deuteronomy 5:16*

HEY!

Want some good (but tough) guidelines for dealing with your parents? Follow the advice given in Ephesians 4:29-32—not just with your parents but with brothers and sisters, too.

JUST DO IT:

If things have been tough between you and your parents lately, find your own bridge, your own park bench. Ask them for some time to talk, to try to work through the problems.

They may be reluctant if they think you're just looking for an excuse to argue, so assure them that you're upset about the way things have been going and you want the chance to work on them together. When they give you that chance, do more listening than talking, and try hard to understand what your parents are saying. Ask them, too, how they're *feeling* about the way things are going.

If things are good between you and your parents, look for a chance today to express some appreciation for what they've done for you.

Give them a chance.

Need more help in handling the hassles in your house? Read Ken's book *How to Live with Your Parents Without Losing Your Mind.* It'll really help!

THERE IS A PRICELESS MASTERPIECE IN YOUR ROOM

When I was a kid, every time the church doors opened we were there. And I didn't *want* to be there. In fact, I was embarrassed to be seen anywhere. I weighed 110 pounds, and I had terminal acne.

My parents spent a fortune on Stridex medicated pads. They don't work—I know, because I ate two of those things every morning for six years.

One morning, my Sunday school teacher looked out over the class with a big smile and said, "God made you!"

God *made me this way?* What happened? Was he experimenting that day? I could just see it. God walks into his workshop and he says, "Today, I think we'll try something different. We'll take a little of this, and mix it with some of this—" And then, when he saw what he had created, he said, "Oh, gross!"

But, hey—I'm not the only one who ever thought they were formed by God on a bad day, right? Many of us have low self-images, and the only way to have a low self-image is to think that God screwed up. One girl told me that she thought God must have sneezed when he was putting her nose on. So you need to hear this: God never made a gross thing in his life. The word "geek" does not exist in God's dictionary.

But standing there, a scrawny 110-pounder with a pizza face, I felt that God had either made a mistake with me or else had decided to punish me for some reason, maybe some obscene gesture I had accidentally made while I was still in the womb. And that's why I didn't have a big, strong body, and athletic ability, and brains.

But that's not the truth.

Here's the truth:

God doesn't make mistakes. And God doesn't design people as cruel punishment for some past sin.

Before the foundation of the earth was put in place, God had your picture on his wall. He knew your name and every contour of your skin, every inflection of your voice. *You* are his masterpiece, designed and built exactly as he wanted to build you, perfect to bring glory to him, and destined to someday be like him.

Hard to believe sometimes? Well, if you think I'm just blowing hot air, read today's verse. You were made from God's blueprint—and then he broke the mold, because he never made another one just like you. Rare paintings and stamps sell for millions. You're worth much more than that—because you're a one-of-a-kind son or daughter of God.

Rejoice!

VERSE OF THE DAY:

For he chose us in him before the creation of the world to be holy and blameless in his sight. In love he predestined [planned ahead for] us to be adopted as his sons through Jesus Christ, in accordance with his pleasure and will.

—*Ephesians 1:4, 5*

HEY!

Psalm 139 is one of the clearest and strongest statements in the Bible that God made us just the way he wants us, and that we're okay. Read it all!

JUST DO IT:

Go to the mirror and take a look. Go on! Take this book with you.

Now—what is it you don't like about the way you're made? Too tall, too short, can't sing, not shaped right, not smart enough? Or maybe it's nothing specific—maybe you just feel that you'd have been better off if you were somebody else. Write on a piece of paper what you wish you could change about yourself. Then pray about it—and try to listen as God tells you why he made you the way he did.

Now look in the mirror and thank God for making you the way he did. Believe me, you don't want to be like someone else! Then plan to use that marvelous creation to bring him glory today—to the max!

ANOTHER NIGHT WITH THE FROGS

Picture this: One day, there are frogs everywhere. His first clue comes early in the morning, when he wakes up to find hundreds of frogs in his bed. When he leaps from the bed, he slips on the thousands of frogs squirming and jumping across the floor.

He investigates and finds that the river near his home has overflowed with frogs; they have spread across the fields, across the roads—even his house is filled with frogs.

All of the other government officials are experiencing the same thing. When the pizza they order is delivered, it's littered with the carcasses of more frogs. Others lie smoldering in the oven.

By the end of the day, he and his friends can't even walk without squashing hundreds of frogs. They're constantly brushing the clinging amphibians from their bodies. But he knows what the problem is—he has been keeping innocent captives as slaves, and the frogs are part of God's "incentive" to make him free them. He also knows who can intercede with God for him to solve this problem. Quickly, he tells a couple of his employees to go find the two men who can make the frogs go away.

When the two men arrive, they offer a deal: They'll make the frogs disappear, but in return he has to promise to set their friends free.

They have him over a barrel and he knows it, so he promises what they ask. When he does, they ask the crucial question: When does he want the frogs to disappear?

And his answer is incredible: "Do it tomorrow."

Tomorrow! You've got to be kidding! If I have frogs smoldering in my pizza and slithering in my pajamas, I want them gone today, right now, this minute—not tomorrow.

True story. Really! The man with the frogs in his pajamas who held innocent people as slaves was Pharaoh, the ruler of ancient Egypt. The slaves were the Israelites. And the men of God who could stop the plague were Moses and his brother Aaron.

Why would Pharaoh want to spend another night with the frogs? Before you decide that maybe ancient people had brain damage, think about this: I've lost track of the number of teenagers I've met who were miserable because they needed to experience forgiveness and a change of heart—two things that are readily available in Jesus Christ. A simple confession, an apology, and a change in attitude was all it would have taken for them to start their way back to the Lord and end that situation or that relationship that was causing them misery.

But some of them have put that decision off for years.

Another night with the frogs.

VERSE OF THE DAY:

For [God] says, "In the time of my favor I heard you, and in the day of salvation I helped you." I tell you, now is the time of God's favor, now is the day of salvation.   *—2 Corinthians 6:2*

HEY!

We didn't make up the story about the frogs. Honest! Read it for yourself in Exodus 8:1-10. And if you like that, read the blood story, and the fly story, and the locust story, and all the rest of the cool "plague" stories in chapters 7 to 12 of Exodus—all part of the fascinating encounter with the man who put if off till tomorrow.

JUST DO IT:

How about you? Are you in a situation you need to get out of? Are you putting off turning your life over to Christ, even though you're sick of the frogs in your life? Make your move today. Allow God to clean out of your life whatever frogs are plaguing you.

Don't spend another night with the frogs.

I'm always amazed at the lengths people will go to to avoid believing in God.

Some of the greatest scientists who've ever lived have essentially said, "I don't care how real or how factual the Scriptures are, I still won't believe them."

Why would anyone run from truth? Possibly because if the story of the Scriptures is true, then we have no reasonable alternative but to worship the God of those Scriptures. And, sadly, mankind will choose almost anything to avoid that. We often choose to live with dishonesty before we'll live with God.

"I DON'T BELIEVE IN YOU, GOD!"

The human race has gone through dozens of philosophies trying to explain our existence, trying to explain where the world came from, and how it works, and what it all really means, and trying to do it leaving out God. Because if God is who he says he is, and if he has done what he says he has done, then we should fall on our faces and worship him.

When man tries to understand his existence, he usually starts with an unspoken assumption: "I don't want to worship God. So I will simply eliminate God from the equation." So we come up with one faulty and untrue philosophy or religion after another, in the mad attempt to avoid the one true God.

There isn't a rational philosophy on the face of the earth that can explain the reason for our existence unless it includes God in its explanation. And when man had worked himself through so many of them that it became clear he would *never* be able to explain existence adequately without including God, then he said, "All right—I'll accept life *without* purpose. Man exists—and that's all there is. There's no design, no meaning whatsoever to life. You're born, you live, you die. End of story. We are like animals, and life is a cruel joke."

And that sad philosophy, called *existentialism,* is the philosophy of the culture you live in today. It teaches that there are no absolutes and there is no meaning. It's one last, desperate attempt to explain life without God.

Think about it for a minute. "Nothing has meaning." It's a great philosophy until you say it! Listen:

"There are no absolutes."

That's an absolute! If there are none, how can you say that?

"Nothing has meaning. And I mean it!"

"There is no right or wrong. And I'm right about that."

Do you hear the problem with that kind of thinking? When you say "Nothing has meaning," you've just made a meaningful statement! How can you do that if nothing has meaning? Even expressing this philosophy violates it! And that points out the difficulty of trying to explain a world that God created without including him in the explanation: The only way to do it is by stating nonsense.

Everything that we see in the universe calls us back to God. The only way to escape him is by retreating not into meaning but into lack of meaning; not into sense but into nonsense; not into hope but into hopelessness.

VERSE OF THE DAY:

The heavens declare the glory of God;
the skies proclaim the work of his hands. —Psalm 19:1

HEY!

Here are some verses you've really got to read that will tell you how people got into the muddled philosophical mess they're in: Romans 1:19-21.

JUST DO IT:

Read the third chapter of John.

Is the loving God portrayed in that chapter a God you would want to ignore or run away from? Doesn't it make far more sense to acknowledge and worship him as creator of the universe?

I magine this:
You're walking home from school or church one day. As you turn the corner and get ready to cross the railroad tracks, there's a guy standing there, right in the middle of the tracks. His clothes are dirty and ripped; he's got one shoe on and one shoe off; his face and arms are bruised and dirty and bleeding.

GET OFF THE TRACKS!

And as you rush toward him to help, he's crying out, "I'm afraid! I'm afraid!"

"Why are you afraid?" you shout.

"A train hit me," he replies, "and I'm afraid another one's gonna do it again!"

What would you tell that man? The same thing any sane person would tell him. "Get off the tracks, dummy! Take three steps sideways, and no train can hit you!"

That story doesn't seem very realistic, of course, because we don't think anybody could be that dumb. But here's one of the saddest truths in the world: Even though God loved us so much that he sent his son Jesus to die on the cross for us so that he could bury our sins in the depths of the earth and forgive us, we spend a major portion of our time dragging those sins back up to the surface so we can play with them one more time. And that's tragic.

Let me illustrate what I mean. A young man came up to me after one of my concerts and said, "I struggle with my thought life—I can't seem to get rid of lustful thoughts." So we prayed together. The next day I walked into the drugstore and there he was by the magazine rack, checking out all the porno mags. I wanted to say to him, "Get off the tracks! If you're struggling with your thought life, move!"

For some of us, it's lustful thoughts and porno mags. For others, it's a group of friends whose influence on us is harmful to our Christian life, but we just can't stay away from them. For others, it might be alcohol or drugs—we want to quit, but for some reason we always find ourselves at those parties where there's plenty of those things to be had. For each of us, it's something.

183

And we'll continue to struggle with those things as long as we don't have the courage or the brains to take three steps sideways and get off the tracks.

I know—it's not that simple. If I'm honest, I'll have to admit that I've spent my share of time sitting there on those tracks. It's hard to tell the friends you've been hanging around with that you can't hang around with them anymore. It's hard to tell the guys you usually drink with that you won't be drinking with them anymore. It's hard to stop watching or reading material that pollutes your mind. Those decisions take courage. Living the Christian life, making the tough decisions we sometimes need to as Christians—that's hard.

But at least God was honest with us. He never said it would be easy. Just the opposite. But Jesus faced the same temptations that we do and resisted them. And he'll help us do the same.

So don't say it's impossible. With God's help, you can get off the tracks.

VERSE OF THE DAY:

No temptation has seized you except what is common to man. And God is faithful; he will not let you be tempted beyond what you can bear. But when you are tempted, he will also provide a way out so that you can stand up under it.
—1 Corinthians 10:13

HEY!

Don't hang around waiting for the train. Read James 4:7.

JUST DO IT:

What are the "railroad tracks" you need to get off—the things that are hurting your Christian life, the sins you keep digging up to play with again? It might be too discouraging to try to take them all on at once, so today pick just one—something you know you should turn away from, and that you know you'll be tempted with today. Determine in your heart—and in your prayers—to resist that temptation today. Then watch for the way of escape he provides. Remember: It is his power, not yours, that will make it possible.

Make up your mind for one day only—and then, tomorrow, make up your mind to do the same thing for one more day.

Wouldn't it have been great to be in Nineveh when Jonah showed up there? Just imagine it: Jonah gets to the city and starts walking down the street. His flesh is all bleached out from being in that fish. He's got seaweed hanging on him. (That's true! It's in the Bible!) The guy smells like whale barf!

And remember—Nineveh wasn't exactly Disneyland. In fact, it was known for its gross sins and cruelty. The Ninevites loved their sins, and they loved to make war on other nations and wipe them out.

So Jonah stops on the street corner, looks around him at all of those cruel warriors, thieves, and prostitutes, and he thinks, *Even God couldn't save this scum. Just to be fair, he sent me to warn them—but after they reject me, he's going to wipe them out! And it will serve them right!*

So Jonah started shouting, "Repent! Stop being bad people! If you don't, God will destroy this whole city, and all of you along with it!"

One man alone. Not an army of evangelists, not an organization, not even a pair of committed believers. Just one man who finally gave in to God and reluctantly said he'd do what God wanted him to do, doubting that it would make any difference anyway.

And that whole ungodly city repented.

Jonah was amazed! In fact, at first he was angry. He thought God should destroy the city because it was so wicked. But God had sent Jonah there to call the people to repentance so that he could *save* the city, not destroy it.

Jonah didn't think he had it in him to cause a whole city to repent. And frankly, he didn't. It was God who caused Nineveh to repent, because God was powerful enough to accomplish what he called Jonah to do. And God is powerful enough to accomplish what he calls *you* to do.

You may not want to do it.

You may think that even if you do, it won't make any difference to anybody.

But if you take a deep breath and dive in, God will do his part.

Just ask Jonah.

VERSE OF THE DAY:

I can do everything through him who gives me strength. —*Philippians 4:13*

HEY!

Read all about the man who walked on water, in Matthew 14:25-33.

JUST DO IT:

If you've read the verse of the day and Matthew 14:25-33, answer these five questions:

1. What was the source of Peter's ability to walk on the water?
2. Why did Peter sink?
3. What was the source of the powerful effect of Jonah's message?
4. Where will you find the source of power to live in obedience to God?
5. When are you going to "go for it"?

"And if I ever get any more gas bills like *this*—" The man waved the envelope in his daughter's face and went on shouting. "That's *it*! No more credit card!"

His daughter and I, both of us in high school at the time, were good friends. But I'd overheard so many arguments like

TREASURE IN YOUR CLOSET

DAVE

that between her and her parents, I'd have to have been crazy not to know that her spending habits were a problem. And frankly, they bothered me, too. It wasn't just how much she spent on gasoline; the amount she spent in a month on clothes, perfume, records, and gadgets of one kind or another was more than I spent in a year. It seemed inconsistent with her Christianity. Was it good for her? Or was it just my own jealousy, since I didn't have much to spend myself?

So I watched for a chance to talk to her about it. That chance came one night when I picked her up for a concert and she asked, as we walked toward the car, how I liked her new dress.

"Looks great," I said—thinking more about how great she looked in it than how the dress looked. "Where'd you get it?"

She told me and I whistled. "Must have been expensive."

She chuckled. "Don't ask."

Now or never, I thought, backing out of the driveway. "I wonder sometimes—is all of this stuff too important to you? I mean, it's coming between you and your parents, who aren't Christians. Wouldn't it be better to spend less and improve your relationship with them so that they'll listen more when you talk about Jesus? All this stuff can become more important to you than God."

She looked hurt, but she laughed it off. "Oh, don't make such a big deal out of it. My parents don't really mean it. Besides, I'm not that attached to this stuff. I buy it because we can afford it. But if I had to leave it behind—" She snapped her fingers. "I could do it just like that."

Could she? I wondered. "'Where your treasure is, there your heart will be also,'" Jesus said in Matthew 6:21. Could she so easily leave behind or give away the possessions she had angered her parents by buying? Unless Jesus was wrong, her heart was hanging in her closet.

I never found out. Over the next year, her spiritual life deteriorated until there was no longer any question of her giving up *anything* for God—and then I lost track of her.

Was her attachment to material possessions the cause of her spiritual problems? I don't know. Maybe it was just another symptom of a deeper problem. But the Bible tells us pretty clearly in today's verse that we become attached to the things we treasure.

How attached am I to material things? There's nothing wrong with making plans for my future, and nothing wrong with owning things. But how much time do I spend planning and scheming—and shopping? How much time maintaining and playing with the things I already own? Is there any time for God when I'm all done? If not, or if the Lord gets just the tail end of my day—the leftovers when I've portioned the rest of it out to all the things that own me—then something has come between me and God.

If I knew that Christ would return for us five minutes from now, would I be dismayed at all the things I'd be leaving behind?

Where's my heart?

VERSE OF THE DAY:

Do not store up for yourselves treasures on earth, where moth and rust destroy, and where thieves break in and steal. But store up for yourselves treasures in heaven, where moth and rust do not destroy, and where thieves do not break in and steal. For where your treasure is, there your heart will be also.   —Matthew 6:19-21

HEY!

Want to know why Jesus called those who acquire lots of possessions "fools"? Read Luke 12:13-21.

JUST DO IT:

Time to take inventory. What do you own that you'd be reluctant to give up, even for God? Don't be afraid to admit it. Make a list of your most valued possessions, and then pretend someone has asked you to give them up, one at a time, for God's sake. Could you do it? What feelings does just thinking about it create in you?

Now reread today's verses. Time for a re-evaluation?

In a commercial jetliner one night at thirty thousand feet in the air, I had sunk as far as I believed a man could go. My family was in jeopardy; my ministry was in jeopardy; I even felt like my soul was in jeopardy. The struggle and the pain in my heart were so bad that I even wondered if life was worth living.

That night I prayed a dangerous, terrible prayer: "God, I don't want to be a Christian anymore! I do want to go to heaven. But I don't want to have to live the Christian life. I want to turn my back on the cross and run. I am tied down by a family that doesn't realize that I'm famous and that I'm a wonderful person. I am tied down by a religion that is not respected by the people that I want to impress. I am tied down by a Holy Spirit who will not free me to enjoy sin. I don't want to be a Christian!"

My pain was so great, sitting in the airplane that night, that I felt like shouting out that prayer. I didn't—they'd have tied me up until the plane landed.

But fortunately, even in my pain, God led me to end my prayer the way Jonah ended his when he was in the belly of that whale:

"You brought my life up from the pit,
    O Lord my God.
When my life was ebbing away,
    I remembered you, Lord,
and my prayer rose to you."

And so I added this to my prayer: "God, I know I'm wrong. So if you want me to want you, you've got to *make* me want you." With tears in my eyes, I whispered, "Please help me, God."

Then I sat there waiting for lightning to strike the plane. The thought crossed my mind that, just as Jonah was almost responsible for the deaths of all of those sailors on that ship thousands of years ago, I would be responsible for the deaths of all the passengers on that plane. (What would I have done if they had cried out, "Who has angered God and caused him to send this storm?" I don't think I'd have said, "God has sent this storm because I am fleeing from him. Throw me out of the plane and you will be saved. God will cause a great bird to pluck me out of the sky!")

It would have made a great story, but no lightning struck. Instead, the guy next to me whipped a dumb little book out of his pocket and tried to witness to me. I'll never forget the look on his face, because to my shame I cursed that man horribly. I said, "You rotten little—Get away from me! I'm already a Christian!"

He didn't have a book for that one!

That man did leave me alone. But later, at the car rental booth at the airport, he tapped me on the shoulder and said, "I just came back to apologize. Sometimes I'm so anxious to share the Good News that I forget to be sensitive." Then he wrote down his phone number and said, "I really do care."

I never called him. He never called me. But after he left me that day, I wept until I was weak.

That was the first step among many that led me back to the Cross.

God doesn't give up on us; he continues to pursue us to the end. Why do I tell you this story? Because not all of your life will be like the last day of church camp, when everyone is hugging you and saying, "Don't forget—live like a Christian! I'll be praying for you!" Not all of your life will be like the first day you turned your life over to Jesus Christ, when you were so happy and relieved you wanted to run out and tell everyone the good news. The feelings of those times fade, and sometimes disappear altogether. And when the good feelings fade and discouragement sets in, that's when we sometimes turn in frustration away from God, when we sometimes think it was a mistake to follow him in the first place. That's when we run from God and pray prayers like, "I don't want to be a Christian anymore!" And that's why one of my favorite verses in the entire Bible is that first verse of the third chapter of Jonah: "Then the word of the Lord came to Jonah a second time."

Maybe you've turned your back on God, turned away from Jesus hanging on the cross for your sins, and chosen instead a boyfriend or a girlfriend, or money, or popularity, or drugs or alcohol, or clothes. And because of that, you're afraid to turn back to him. I want to tell you joyfully today that when you turn back to God, you won't find a fist. You'll find him standing, waiting, saying, "Are you ready now? I give you a second chance."

God gave Jonah a second chance; God gave me a second chance; God will give you a second chance.

But first you have to stop running away, turn around, and accept it.

VERSE OF THE DAY:

I love the Lord, for he heard my voice;
he heard my cry for mercy.
Because he turned his ear to me,
I will call on him as long as I live.   *—Psalm 116:1, 2*

HEY!

King David, who often experienced God's forgiveness and mercy, knew he couldn't hide from God. Read about it in Psalm 139:7-12.

JUST DO IT:

Today's Jumper Fable is for anyone who, for whatever reason, wants to cry out to God. Just do it.

Angry? Tell him so. Experiencing grief because of a loss? He wants to hear about it. Discouraged and depressed? Tell him. He'll hear your cry and he will answer. You may not see lightning or hear a booming voice, but he cares and he will respond to you.

Believe it.

PLAYING BY THE RULES

Here's a unique initiation rite used by one group of Boy Scouts: The boy to be initiated was led blindfolded into the forest and taken to an old deserted cabin with a dirt floor. When the whole group was assembled in the cabin, the one being initiated was told that the cabin contained an old dry well into which many a careless boy scout had fallen.

To prove their point, the boys would hand their blindfolded friend a stone, telling him to carefully lean out and drop it into the well. Of course, there *was* no well, but the boys knew how to convince their friend that there was. When he dropped the stone, one of the other boys would silently catch it. After a couple of seconds, a third boy would drop a stone in the far corner of the old dirt floor. To the blindfolded boy, it sounded like a very deep well. He was then told that he had to wait alone in the cabin for thirty minutes. If he removed his blindfold or if he fell into the well, he would not be allowed to join. Then the boys would leave the cabin and watch from outside.

The blindfolded boy left behind would suddenly be surrounded by a scary silence. Most of the boys who went through this initiation would simply sit, frozen in fear, until their friends returned. They must have been curious to know more about the cabin they were in; they must have been tempted to scoot around a little or to feel around them, even blindfolded—but they didn't dare. Why? Because they didn't know where the holes were.

The joke, of course, was on them. There *were* no holes. It was just an adolescent prank. But in real life, the holes are many and deadly. To warn us about those holes, we have rules.

Some people hate rules and prefer to ignore them. But life isn't an adolescent prank—the holes are real. And those who ignore the rules might just fall into one of those holes. The pilot who refuses to follow the guidelines of safety or the rules of flight will die and probably take others with him. The surgeon who disregards the rules of medicine will hurt rather than heal. And men and women who decide that the moral rules of life don't apply to them will pay a price for their error.

Most of us don't like rules. We think they limit our freedom. We wish God hadn't given us so many absolute moral laws: No sex before marriage; obey your parents; no lying or stealing. But those rules serve a purpose that makes great common sense—they protect us from making some mistakes that God knows will hurt us.

The guidelines that he gave us were designed not to imprison us but to set us free. Rebelling against those guidelines is very costly. Like the pilot who refuses to trust the instruments, or the ship's captain who refuses to use the compass, we find ourselves in tremendous peril.

Do you want to live a life of freedom? You don't do that by throwing the rule book out the window. You do that by acknowledging that life is full of dangerous holes and using the rule book to avoid them.

People who throw the rules out the window throw away their potential at the same time. Some run wildly, thinking that at last they're free—until they fall into those holes and are destroyed. Other live in timid fear because they don't know where the holes are.

It is common in today's society to deny that there are any moral absolutes, and that trend has cost us dearly. The sexual revolution, for instance, didn't lead to freedom; it led to fear and death. We ignored the rules, and now we're paying the price.

The truly creative musician is not one who understands nothing of the discipline of music and plays without form or reason. The creative musician is one who so thoroughly understands and masters the discipline of music that she is free to improvise and bring individual beauty to the form.

The successful athlete is not the one who refuses to train and discipline his body and doesn't bother to learn the fundamentals of his sport. The athletes who astound us with their skill are those who are so disciplined in the basics of their sport that they can react to unusual and demanding situations as easily as I would tie my shoe. (Or maybe even better; my shoe keeps coming untied.)

The one who's living life fully isn't the one who runs around wildly, disregarding moral values and spitting in the face of God. The one who's living life fully is the one who delights in the laws that guide us to life and is therefore free to operate at peak performance within the freedom-producing guidelines set forth by the Creator.

VERSE OF THE DAY:

Praise the Lord.
Blessed is the man who fears the Lord,
who finds great delight in his commands.   —Psalm 112:1

If your law had not been my delight,
I would have perished in my affliction.   —Psalm 119:92

HEY!

Read all of Psalm 119 to see how God's laws are designed to bring joy to our life.

JUST DO IT:

Are there some of God's rules you've chosen to ignore? If so, and if you realize that you're putting yourself at risk by ignoring those rules, now's the time to start living by them again. If you just don't think it's worth it to "give up your freedom" (even though, in the end, by following the rules you really *gain* freedom), take our advice: Make an appointment with a Christian counselor you can trust and talk it over. Because the risk is great, it doesn't hurt to have a second opinion.

I should have stayed in bed.
It was the day of the hand/eye coordination test in my high-school gym class. Each student would be required to catch a football three times, each time running in a different direction. And the final grade for the semester would rest on how well we performed.

DROPPING THE BALL

I knew I was in trouble. I had the hand/eye coordination of a carp. Because of a physical deformity—curvature of the bone in both arms that restricted my movement—I couldn't catch a football while standing still, let alone while running. I can still feel the humid breath of stale air that hung over the athletic field that day. I can see how it stirred the sandy hair of the boy in front of me. His name was Daniel, but he was built like Hercules. He had muscles in places I didn't even have places. He stepped forward to take his turn, and I swallowed hard, knowing that I'd be next. Daniel ran to the left and caught the ball thrown by the instructor. He also caught the next ball, thrown to the right. Then he ran down the field, full speed, for the long pass. He watched over his shoulder as the ball spiraled toward him, then he reached up at the last possible moment and snatched it from the air. The momentum of the ball caused him to stumble, but he quickly regained his balance and, with one hand, waved the ball above his head in victory.

I couldn't even hold the ball in one hand, much less wave it. I heard my name and stepped forward, knowing that I couldn't catch that ball. At that moment, I wished that my physical deformity were more noticeable so that the young P.E. instructor would be more sympathetic. As it was, his intensity made it seem that passing this test was a life-and-death matter.

The first ball actually hit my hands as I stumbled to the left. I thought that was pretty miraculous in itself. Unfortunately, I couldn't turn my palms flat enough to pull it in.

As I ran to the right, I almost caught it. In slow motion, the ball danced at the end of my outstretched hands, tempting me with success. Then it fell to the ground about the same time I did.

I never even saw the long pass until it was bouncing in front of me.

"Hit the showers," the instructor growled without looking at me. "You'll never amount to anything."

You'll never amount to anything.

If he had known the effect those words would have, I don't think he would ever have said them. I tried to block out the laughter of my classmates as I walked the one hundred miles to that locker-room door. Inside, I was grateful for the cascading water that camouflaged my tears. Probably what that instructor meant was that I'd never make a good football player, but in my mind his words applied to my entire life. I didn't think of his words as cruel. I thought of them as true. How could anyone with his authority and athletic ability be wrong? I wept not because I couldn't catch a football; I wept because I thought I lacked some valuable ingredient in my life that God had graciously bestowed on most other people but had forgotten or neglected to give to me. I was measuring my worth by a false standard, and I didn't measure up. I couldn't run fast, I was uncomfortable with the opposite sex, I wasn't athletic, I wasn't exceptionally bright. And I really believed what my coach told me: I would never amount to anything.

And I began that day a quest to prove to myself and to everyone else that I was worth something, that my life had some redeeming value. It's a quest that you may be on as well; it's a quest that many young people set out on. And it's a quest that begins on a foundation of quicksand.

Why do people set out to prove their worth? Because they're trying to disprove their own secret belief that they are indeed worthless. Deep down, even before my coach's comment, I already saw myself as worthless. It would be years before I would begin to understand what actually gave my life its value, and in the meantime the search would cost me much wasted time, personal agony, and missed opportunities.

People who are aware of their own worth and of why they have that value, have nothing to prove to anybody. Instead, they demonstrate with their lives every day, without particularly trying to, what they already know to be true—that God loves them and has an important role for them to play in life, a role for which he first designed and then created them. And the God who created us doesn't make junk.

Then that same God freely gave his own Son so that our sins could be forgiven. First by creating us, and second by giving his own Son to save us, God has bestowed incredible value on each one of us—on me and on you. To try to prove our worth in any other way is to insult everything God has done for us.

People who understand this demonstrate to those around them that they are important, capable, and loved.

I didn't discover that truth about myself until years later. I wish I had known it that day, crying in the showers.

You don't have to wait that long. You can know it today.

VERSE OF THE DAY:

"For I know the plans I have for you," declares the Lord, "plans to prosper you and not to harm you, plans to give you hope and a future." —Jeremiah 29:11

HEY!

Here's more about how much God loves us: 1 John 3:1-3.

JUST DO IT:

Spend some time today quietly praying and meditating. Ask God to show you the areas in your life about which you feel unworthy; ask him to show you how you're trying to demonstrate your worth to the people around you.

You may indeed have failed in some significant ways, but that has nothing to do with your worth. You are worthy because of how much God loves you, because of what he has already done for you, because of the plans he has for your life—not because of anything you've accomplished. And that's a great thing because it frees you from the burden of having to succeed in some obvious way so that you can prove your worth. When you feel you have to prove your worth to everyone, you're living for the approval of those around you. Once you accept the approval God offers you, you're free to live for God. Accept that gift today.

LEARNING ABOUT THE BIRDS AND THE BEES— AND THE COWS

I learned about sex from my cousin. We were walking down a road throwing stones at the birds lined up on the telephone wires, when we came to a field full of cattle. Close to the road, a bull was breeding a cow. We rolled on the ground and laughed until I thought my sides would split.

Why were we laughing? What was so funny? I admit that a bull breeding a cow is not a particularly pretty sight, and neither is it a high moment in comedy. Looking back, I think I was laughing because I felt confused and stupid. I grew up on a farm, so I had seen this before—without laughing. I had even helped with the delivery of several calves, which deep down inside had stirred a curiosity about my own sexual make-up. But believe it or not, until that day with my cousin, I had never put two and two together. (Don't laugh! I'm sure I'm not the only one who's ever been that dense when it comes to sex. In fact, I remember reading a couple of years ago about a nurse who didn't know she was pregnant until the baby arrived! Surprise!) It was easier to laugh that day than to reveal my ignorance and risk being laughed at.

After the bull had completed his performance and we had exhausted all the crude comments we could think of, my cousin turned to me and said, "That's what your father did to your mother to get you."

I hit him in the face. As he fell to the ground, I was right on top of him, pounding with both fists. "Don't you ever say that about my mom and dad!" I screamed.

He started to laugh at me. The more he insisted it was true, the madder I got. All my life I had thought of sex as something crude and dirty. My parents weren't crude and dirty, nor were they cows, so how could he say they would do such a thing?

Before long, of course, I discovered that my cousin was right. But those first impressions of sex—that it was something to be sneered and laughed at—stayed with me for a long, long time.

For much of my youth, I was certain that someone besides God had created sex. I thought that God gave us all the normal stuff, and then when he took a coffee break, Satan snuck in and gave us the sex organs and all the feelings that make them work. What else can you think when you believe that sex is dirty? And, I must admit, there were times when that feeling was reinforced by the teaching of well-meaning Christians who, out of their frustration at seeing lives destroyed by the misuse of sex, tried to protect me by teaching me that sex was dirty so that I would avoid it altogether. But that, too, is a misuse of sex, and it, too, can destroy lives.

The truth is: God made sex, and he made it enjoyable so that it would be enjoyed by the creatures he loves so much. It is one of the greatest expressions of love that two people can share. But man has twisted God's creation. Instead of acknowledging that God made sex and following his guidelines for its use, we have made sex our god and allow our lives to revolve around it.

Some cultures put likenesses of their gods everywhere. So do we—we put sex everywhere. It's on almost all advertising billboards, on nearly every television show, rarely missing from the movies and plays you watch, and it's the major subject of conversation at most schools. In the midst of all that, is it possible to find a balanced view of sex that doesn't deny our own sexuality and yet doesn't emphasize sex at the expense of everything else?

Yes, it is—if you do two things:

First, keep your understanding of the importance of sex in balance. It's important, but it isn't *all-important*. It isn't more important than the God who made both you and sex. It isn't more important than living for him.

And second, remember that he made it. If he made it, you can bet that he had a plan for how it's to be used, just as Abner Doubleday, who invented baseball, had certain rules in mind that make the game more fun and easier to play without war erupting between the teams. God's plan for sex is in the Bible—which, I suppose, makes the Bible a sort of sex manual.

Followed carefully and joyfully, that plan of God's can make sex one of the greatest joys of your life. Ignore God's plan, and sex will become a source of great heartache for you.

You see, God didn't give us rules about sex to ruin our fun. Why would he do that? He gave us sex for our enjoyment. He gave us the rules because he knew how sex works best, and he knew that if we misused it, we'd pay a horrible price.

He gave us the rules because he loves us and only wants what's best for us.

Play by the rules.

VERSE OF THE DAY:

God created man in his own image,…male and female he created them.…God saw all that he had made, and it was very good. —Genesis 1:27, 31

HEY!

God didn't give us a long list of rules about sex, but the ones he did give us are pretty important. Get an idea of how important in 1 Corinthians 6:9-20.

JUST DO IT:

Time to make sure you understand just what God's rules are about sex. But that's not the purpose of this book. There are many ways to find out, though. Here are a couple of suggestions:

First, ask an adult you're comfortable with and can trust just what God's standards for sex are. Sure, you know some of them already, but you might find out something you don't know.

Second, read a book about it. Ken's book *I Don't Remember Dropping the Skunk, But I Do Remember Trying to Breathe* (Grand Rapids: Zondervan Publishing House, 1990) has some chapters about sex and dating. And here are a couple of others:

Handling Your Hormones: The "Straight Story" on Love and Sexuality, Revised Edition, by Jim Burns. (Eugene, Oregon: Harvest House, 1986).

Next Time I Fall in Love: How to Handle Sex, Intimacy, and Feelings in Dating Relationships, by Chap Clark (Grand Rapids: Zondervan Publishing House, 1987).

I probably shouldn't be down here, Gary thought, twisting onto his back and inching through a damp muddy passage on his shoulder blades. A cardinal rule of spelunkers—never enter a cave alone. But it was his last day in the area, and he hadn't been able to find a partner. It was now, alone—or never.

A WORLD WITHOUT LIGHT

DAVE

He was probably a half-mile into the cave, his only light source the carbon-powered headlamp strapped to his forehead to keep his hands free for climbing. He scrambled out of the narrow passage into a huge cavern so big that his light couldn't even reach the far wall or the ceiling. Chocolate-brown stalactites hung out of the blackness; crystals twinkled on a nearby wall. "Wow," he breathed.

Halfway across the cavern he stopped short—a great pit, a dozen feet wide, yawned at his feet. He kicked a loose rock into the blackness. Silence. He kicked in another, and waited half a minute. Silence. "Guess I'll skip that part of the tour," he said, then listened to his own echoes. He sat at the pit's rim. His carbon lamp was getting dim—time to put in a new carbon pellet. Out of his pack he pulled the little jar of pellets, opened it, and set it on the rock near him. Then he removed his headlamp, took one last look around, and shut it off, plunging the cave into utter blackness. By feel, his eyes useless because of the complete lack of light, he opened the lamp and tossed aside the old pellet. Then he reached for the jar of new pellets—and knocked it over with his groping fingers, spilling the pellets down the sloping rock floor into the pit. In a panic he grabbed for the jar—and sent it spinning into the chasm. One or two last pellets rattled down the slope and dropped into nothingness, and then the only sound was the rapid pounding of Gary's heart in his ears. Utter blackness.

Even in the icy stillness of that black air deep inside the earth, he could feel the cold sweat popping out on his face as he fought panic. No light, no partner, no way out. He sat motionless a minute or two, concentrating on keeping himself in control. Then he reached out very slowly, his fingers moving at a snail's pace across the smooth rock beside him, all his concentration focused on his fingertips. Something loose there—he stopped and felt it carefully. A piece of gravel. On he groped, slowly—until, at last, his fingers found a tiny, smooth cylinder: one last carbon pellet that had not rolled into the abyss. Fingers shaking, forcing himself to take his time, he inserted it into his lamp, snapped it back together, switched it on—and the cavern was filled with the most glorious thing imaginable: *light*. He held up his fingers and examined them, marveling at the play of light and shadow on the textured surface of his skin. He could see. There was light. A moment before he had expected to die. Now he would live. There was *light*.

It's a true story. It happened years ago to a guy I knew. And every time I heard Gary tell that story, hints of that panic would creep back into his voice as he described his plunge into black hopelessness. You may be thinking, *I know why you're telling that story—because Jesus is the light of the world.* Yes, he is; he said so in John 8:12. But he also said to his followers in Matthew 5:14: "You are the light of the world—let your light shine before men." Jesus wants us to be a light in a dark place. Today's verse encourages us to live a "blameless and pure" life so that we will "shine like stars in the universe." Believe me, in today's society anything blameless and pure is bound to stand out! And because we stand out, because even in our imperfection we represent the light and truth of God, we can illuminate the world around us, just as that tiny pellet in Gary's headlamp lit that huge cavern around him and brought him new hope for life.

Like a light in a dark cave, like a star in a midnight sky, we are to be dramatically and unmistakably different from all around us. Sometimes that's not easy; sometimes that's uncomfortable. But if we don't allow God's light to shine forth through us, we could be keeping in darkness someone who desperately *needs* the light to survive.

Let it shine!

VERSE OF THE DAY:

Do everything without complaining or arguing, so that you may become blameless and pure, children of God without fault in a crooked and depraved generation, in which you shine like stars in the universe. —Philippians 2:14, 15

HEY!

Read that great passage from the Sermon on the Mount, too, where Jesus calls us light and salt: Matthew 5:13-16.

JUST DO IT:

If we really take to heart Jesus' instructions to us in these passages of Scripture, we need to ask ourselves some tough questions: In what ways are we different from those around us? Are we different at all, in any way that people can see? In what ways do we bring light to a dark world? By our words? Our actions? Our attitudes? Is there anyone who is searching for the light we bring with the same desperation that Gary searched for that last carbon pellet?

Set a goal for yourself today. Choose one way in which you will shine forth like a Christian—boldly and brightly. Without fear. Then follow through.

Be a star today.

TOO CLOSE TO THE LINE

I grew up in a very strict background. I grew up with the kind of Christianity that has lots of rules.

I think maybe that's why, when I got a bit older, although I knew what was right and what was wrong, I chose to walk as close to that line between them as I could. "Look at all the liberty I have!" I was saying to the world. "Look at what a cool Christian I am! Here's evil, right here, and I'm nudged right up against it—and I'm still okay!"

What happened next is pretty predictable, I'm afraid. Satan reached out with his tentacles and drew me into sin. And he clouded my mind so that I had a hard time finding that line between right and wrong; some of the decisions I made were the wrong decisions, and they could have destroyed me.

It was only God's grace that kept me from ruining my life during that time, but because of what I learned then, I now have a very different perspective on how a Christian should live. The guidelines and rules of the Bible are not just some good advice for Christians who are too weak to be able to control themselves. They are God's instructions for all of those who follow him, regardless of how weak or how strong.

And I have a different perspective, too, on that line between right and wrong. If one side of that line represents Satan and his attempts to seduce me, and the other side represents God and where he wants me to be, then I want to take about ten giant steps over to God's side—especially in those areas where I know that I'm weak.

"But you could walk right up to that line and still not be sinning," you might be saying.

Yes, I know. But I can walk way over here and be safe. Maybe "safe" doesn't sound all that attractive to you, not very exciting. But when it comes to choosing between good and evil, between God and Satan, safe is just what you want to be.

Be safe. Stay away from the line.

VERSE OF THE DAY:

Listen, my son, accept what I say,
and the years of your life will be many.
I guide you in the way of wisdom
and lead you along straight paths.
When you walk, your steps will not be hampered;
when you run, you will not stumble.
Hold on to instruction, do not let it go;
guard it well, for it is your life.
Do not set foot on the path of the wicked
or walk in the way of evil men.

—Proverbs 4:10-14

HEY!

Here's some sound advice from the book of James; read verse 7, chapter 4.

JUST DO IT:

Make today a day of examining yourself and your life. Are there areas where you're walking too close to the line? Sometimes those areas are easy to spot, sometimes not. Try to find a quiet time during the day to pray and think about your life. Do you have a friend, counselor, or youth pastor who knows you well enough to point out to you the places you risk crossing the line? If so, ask them to help you make this evaluation. Good luck!

OUTNUMBERED TOGETHER

DAVE

I slipped into the back of the first-grade classroom, smiled and nodded at the teacher, and touched my son's shoulder. He hopped up gratefully and followed me out. We were going to lunch.

For me it had been a long morning. My third child, a daughter, had been born just an hour before. Now it was time to reassure my son that his mother and new sister were doing fine and to show him by this special lunch that he hadn't lost his place in our family. But I was worried about one thing: He had wanted a brother.

So, over pizza, I broke the news, trying to keep it as upbeat as possible. And he took it calmly—*too calmly*, I thought. I watched him concentrate on fingernailing all the mushrooms off his slice and wondered how much resentment he might be hiding.

"Well, now that you have two sisters," I said craftily, "I guess you're outnumbered—two to one."

He sipped his Coke and thought it over. Then he shook his head and said quietly, "No, Dad—now we're outnumbered, three to two."

Now we're outnumbered. Sure. After all, who wants to be outnumbered all by himself? End of problem.

I chuckled. And it wasn't until days later, with the new baby safely at home, that the true meaning of what he'd said dawned on me. How many others around me, even in my own family and among my close friends, are outnumbered all by themselves? How many have some unsolvable problem they can tell no one about? Some sin they should confess to ease their guilt? Some worry? Some enemy to withstand?

For my son, in the tiny trauma of being outnumbered by his sisters, it was so easy. Secure in his position in the family, surrounded by people who loved him, he merely reached out and claimed the help of the father he knew would stand by him. Still outnumbered, sure—but not alone.

Do you sometimes feel outnumbered? Maybe you're outnumbered by all the kids at your school who seem to be more popular than you are, or to have more money, or to be better looking or smarter, or better athletes. Maybe you're feeling outnumbered because you're a Christian and you don't know many other Christians. Maybe television and movies and most of the things you read or hear about in school are not only on a different wavelength from your Christian beliefs, they're downright hostile to what you believe. There are plenty of ways to be outnumbered.

Thank God we have a heavenly Father who is more powerful than all of those who outnumber or oppose us put together. Thank God also that we have Christian brothers and sisters who'll stand by us and who make up our family. All we have to do is reach out and grab hold of them and claim their help.

Feeling outnumbered? That's okay. We'll be outnumbered together.

VERSE OF THE DAY

Two are better than one.
If one falls down,
his friend can help him up.
But pity the man who falls
and has no one to help him up!
Also, if two lie down together, they will keep warm.
But how can one keep warm alone?
Though one may be overpowered,
two can defend themselves.
A cord of three strands is not quickly broken.

—Ecclesiastes 4:9-12

HEY!

Even Jesus knew what it was like to be lonely and afraid and in anguish and to need his friends to stand by him. He also knew what it was like when none of them were strong enough to hang in there. Read about it in Mark 14:32-41.

JUST DO IT:

If you've been trying to make it all alone and would like to take advantage of the family you have as a Christian, here are some suggestions:

1. Realize that God the Father is one of your team members. Ask for his power and guidance in the situation you're facing.

2. Find at least one Christian friend who'll stand with you, encourage you, and challenge you to grow in the Lord.

3. Be a friend to others who could use your encouragement. Do something specific: Call them on the phone, talk to them at school, write them a note—something that lets them know they aren't outnumbered all alone—that there's at least one person standing by them.

A KILLER TESTIMONY

I don't have a real fancy testimony like some folks have. I used to wish that I did. I dreamed that they'd introduce me and I would come out and tell about my horrible background: "I killed twenty-eight people with a wet squirrel. I was into drugs. I shot peanut butter into my vein right there. Crunchy peanut butter. It drove me nuts.

"Yeah, I was with a different woman every night, and I was drunk every other night, and then when I was four years old I became a Christian."

I also dreamed of the "hero" testimony: "Yeah, there I was on the two-yard line, ninety-eight yards to go. The gun for the two-minute warning had just sounded, and the score was 131 to 0. Right there I knelt and asked Jesus to come into my life, and you know the rest. We scored 131 points in two minutes and won the Super Bowl in overtime. Of course, after the Super Bowl I went to Disneyland, where I immediately led most of the cartoon characters to Christ."

Don't get me wrong—I think it's wonderful that God changes people's lives like that, but those dramatic testimonies we're so used to hearing are not the only evidence of his power. The simple fact is: All of us are separated from God by our sins, serial killers and normal people alike. Before you go any further, get a Bible and read Romans 3:23. Be sure to keep your Bible open. You'll need it again in just a minute.

Have you read it? See? It isn't just the murderer or child molester who's in need of God's forgiveness. It's *all* of us. Every one of us has a natural tendency to rebel against God.

Now turn to chapter 6, verse 23, of Romans to see how serious all sin is to God. Not only is our sin serious enough to warrant a death penalty, but God cared enough to send his Son to die for us to pay that penalty. And he didn't die only for murderers; he also died for people who just tell little lies. That makes your testimony dramatic whether you're serving a life sentence for terrorism or your worst sin is kicking your brother in the shin. Either way, you've been saved from certain death. It took the death of the Son of God to make up for those sins. He died, he was buried, and he rose again so that you could live.

Don't ever think that your testimony isn't dramatic enough. It's awesome enough to shout to the whole world.

VERSE OF THE DAY:

For God so loved the world that he gave his one and only son, that whosoever believes in him shall not perish but have eternal life. —John 3:16

HEY!

How should we respond to God's great sacrifice for us? Read 1 John 4: 9-12.

JUST DO IT:

There is only one thing to do in the face of such mercy and grace. Can you say "thank you"? I knew you could. Now, the best thank-you of all is to give your life back to him. How can you show him gratitude with your life today?

I t was one of those crazy, how-did-I-get-into-this-mess kind of things that can only happen when you're in high school.

IT ALL DEPENDS

DAVE

I had agreed to go on a blind date, but I decided to call the girl a few days beforehand just so I'd know what to expect.

What a conversation! It didn't take long to figure out that the two of us weren't exactly two peas in a pod. She used slang so new that I hadn't even heard it yet and had no idea what it meant. She laughed loudly and often; I was quiet. She wanted to talk about top-40 music; I liked obscure, alternative music groups she'd never heard of. She mentioned that she never went to church; I went every week. I was glad that she seldom stopped talking, because I was struggling just to keep my end of the conversation going.

Sitting a few feet away from me, thumbing through a comic book as I mumbled into the telephone, was a friend of mine. He laughed every now and then at some clumsy thing I said and offered helpful comments like, "Way to go, Hot Lips."

Out of the blue, after we'd been talking for a few minutes, my future date asked, "Do you swear?"

Up to that point I'd been trying to fool her into thinking that I was the kind of guy she'd enjoy going out with, but now the game was up. The fact was that I didn't think swearing was the best way for a Christian to represent Christ in the world, so I didn't. And I wasn't going to lie about it even though I knew what she was hoping I'd say. "Uh—no, I don't," I said.

"You're kidding."

"Nope."

She was quiet for a few seconds. Then: "Let me talk to your friend."

"Who?"

"The guy who's laughing. Let me talk to him."

So I handed him the phone. He gave me a "watch this" look, tucked the phone against his shoulder, and came on like Mr. Cool. (Meanwhile, I figured out thirteen ways to get out of the date. It wasn't hard—she was as anxious as I was.) After a few opening lines, she asked my friend the same question. "Oh, it all depends," he answered.

"Depends on what?" she asked.

"Depends on who I'm with."

Ain't that the truth, I thought. What a phony. He was a Christian, and it's true that he never swore when we were at church—but I'd heard him swear often enough when he was with his friends at school. Even though he was one of my best friends, I'd never realized until that minute what a double life he led.

But then, who was I to judge? Swearing wasn't a problem for me, but there were plenty of things that were, including the same holier-than-thou attitude I was suddenly feeling toward my friend. When it came to leading a double life, I was a champ. In fact, one of my greatest fears was that my thoughts would suddenly become visible in a little balloon above my head and people would realize what a hypocrite I was.

And I wasn't alone. Each of us has areas of vulnerability in which we have a hard time establishing strong standards of behavior and sticking to them. Oh, sure, we can live by those high standards when we're with people who live by the same standards—our friends from church, maybe, or our parents. But what about when we're with people who scoff at those standards, or who seem to have more fun without them? It all depends on the people we're with. It shouldn't. But it does.

Nobody likes to stand when everybody else is sitting. Nobody likes to be wearing a suit when everybody else is wearing jeans and a T-shirt. Nobody likes to speak Spanish when everybody else is speaking English. Nobody wants to act like heaven when everybody else is acting like Sodom and Gomorrah.

So we become like chameleons—those little lizards that can change their color to blend in with their environment. We take on the appearance and the habits of the people we're with. You see, it's easy to be a Christian when you're around Christians. The tough part, the real test, comes when you go someplace where it's hard to be a Christian, and still hang in there. If, instead of living by "It all depends on who I'm with," you live by "I'll live for God wherever I am, whoever I'm with," you will make a real difference in the world.

Don't be a chameleon Christian. *Stand out!*

VERSE OF THE DAY:

Blessed is the man who perseveres under trial, because when he has stood the test, he will receive the crown of life that God has promised to those who love him.

—James 1:12

HEY!

Does it just seem too hard going against the crowd? Read 1 Peter 5:8, 9.

JUST DO IT:

Don't feel guilty about the times you've lived a double life in the past. Confess it to God, accept his forgiveness, and then move on.

The real question is this: How are you going to keep from living a double life in the future? List at least three ways you'll find the strength to live for God when it's hard, when you're the only one, when you don't really want to.

BETTER THAN SEX

I'm as alive and normal as the next guy. I've got all the same hormones and drives as any other male.

But if I had to choose between never having sexual intercourse again and never having the warm, accepting love that is communicated and demonstrated between my wife and me in hugs, glances, and the quiet moments of just holding each other, I would give up intercourse in a moment.

I can just hear you saying, "No you wouldn't."

Oh, yes, I would.

Now you're saying, "You must be crazy!"

No, I'm not crazy.

Now you're saying, "Yes, but you are old!"

Compared to you I may be old, but my sex drive is alive and well. I'm not saying that sexual intercourse isn't enjoyable or important. I am saying that it is not the most important aspect of marriage, nor does it even come close to being enough to hold a marriage together. Sexual intercourse is only one part of sex. The strongest aspects of love go far beyond the bedroom. Unfortunately, our society doesn't seem to realize that. Society often limits its definition of sex to the act of sexual intercourse. Not true. The beauty of your sexuality started long before you were even aware of the opposite sex, and it continues far beyond the act of intercourse.

When you were a child and first experienced the warm, reassuring touch of your mother and the secure, firm hug of your father, those feelings were a part of your sexual makeup. They were the first building blocks that would later enable you to love and to be loved in a sexual way. Those feelings had nothing to do with being turned on—but they were sexual feelings nevertheless. Later, you terrified your mother and father the first time you discovered your own sexual organs. And those were sexual feelings, too—even though you didn't know what the things you had discovered were for. You shocked your parents because they identified all sexual feelings with eroticism; they couldn't see that you were simply and innocently curious. Then you hit puberty. Your body began to mature sexually, and your hormones began to kick in, and your sexual curiosity gauge buried the needle clear over in the red zone. And much (Okay, let's face it) —*all* of that curiosity has to do with the act of intercourse itself and with the parts of the body associated with it. That's normal, but it's also misleading because sex, as any married couple with a healthy sex life can tell you, involves all the parts of the relationship.

Things always go better in the bedroom when a husband and wife have a healthy friendship and respect and have kept alive all the other elements of love: teasing and laughing together, cards and phone calls and flowers, doing the dishes together, sharing dreams and fears, and so on.

What does that have to do with me? you may be asking. *I'm not married yet.* True. But you're in a good position to begin developing strong friendships, a healthy and positive respect for the members of the opposite sex (which is pretty hard to do if you're mainly concerned with taking advantage of them sexually), and an understanding of all the aspects of love. Those are the things that will best prepare you for happiness in marriage.

Your sexual curiosity is natural. But don't mistake that for the whole show. Watch the happily, affectionately married people you know to see how they behave toward each other in public. Observe the respect, the humor and lightness, the courtesy (opening doors, helping each other in little ways), the gentle looks and touches. Those are things you can begin working on in your relationships with friends of the opposite sex now. And you'll be doing far more than you realize to prepare yourself for that more intense relationship later.

VERSE OF THE DAY:
Marriage should be honored by all, and the marriage bed kept pure, for God will judge the adulterer and all the sexually immoral. —*Hebrews 13:4*

HEY!
How long has it been since you read the story of the first man and woman, Adam and Eve? Read it in Genesis 2:4-25. It really shows the importance of the marriage relationship.

JUST DO IT:

Today, pay attention to the way you interact with the members of the opposite sex around you. Try to imagine how they perceive you, based on your behavior. Do they see you as someone who's always got sex on your mind? Do they see you as someone who's respectful and thoughtful, fun to be around?

If you have a good friend of the opposite sex who can be trusted to be honest and also sympathetic, you might even take a risk and ask him or her what your behavior says about your attitudes.

Think over what you've learned. Do you need to change some attitudes? Some patterns of behavior?

THE PLEASURE PRINCIPLE

DAVE

The serpent laughed, his black scales glistening in the sun. "Die? Do you know why he said that you would die? Because he knows that if you eat the fruit, you will become like him, knowing good from evil."

He curled around the limb, stretched his long neck slowly to the cluster of golden fruit that hung, fragrant, in the crystal air, and licked a drop of dew that hung there. "Eat the fruit," he whispered. "You will not die."

Eve hesitated. Should she not talk first with Adam? But just as she turned to go, the serpent's eyes flashed. She stayed, fascinated by their depth and color. "Touch the fruit and see," he said casually.

She lifted a hand slowly and touched one golden fruit. Never had she felt anything so silky, so smooth, so inviting. It was as soft and warm as her own skin.

And suddenly it was loose in her hand. Had she picked it? She didn't remember. She brought it to her nose. Ah! More fragrant even than the roses she wore in her black hair.

She caught the serpent's eye once more, read the urging there without a word passing between them, and opened her lips. She felt the fruit's skin give beneath her teeth, then the bursting of it, and the indescribable juice flowing onto her tongue and down her chin. And so the deed was done.

Have you ever wondered how Eve could have been so foolish as to actually eat the fruit and disobey God? It seems to us that it would have been so simple and easy to obey. After all, she and Adam could do anything at all except one thing—eat the fruit of one tree.

Maybe the answer is in Genesis 3:6: "When the woman saw that the fruit of the tree was good for food and pleasing to the eye, and also desirable for gaining wisdom, she took some and ate it." According to that verse, there were three reasons Eve ate the fruit. She believed that it would make her wise, as the serpent had said. But she also ate it because it was delicious and beautiful. In other words, it gave her pleasure to hold it and eat it, so she did—regardless of God's command.

And so Eve, to her anguish, became the first to discover the law of human nature that we can call the Pleasure Principle: *When given a choice, we tend to choose the thing that gives us the most pleasure.*

Most of us go through a day the same way we go through a bakery. The doughnuts are on the left, and the whole-wheat bread is on the right—and we choose the doughnuts every chance we get. And what's wrong with that? Is it a sin to enjoy ourselves? Didn't God give us our five senses, and didn't he create the things that we enjoy with them? After all, the Bible never says it's wrong to choose that which is pleasurable, does it?

Yes and no. The Bible clearly teaches that some sins are pleasurable things. Some people apparently find drunkenness to be pleasurable, for instance. Sexual promiscuity must be pleasurable or it wouldn't be such a problem for so many people. Do you like food? So do I. But eating can be overdone, and when it is, it's a sin, too. But this is no surprise, is it? Of course sins are pleasurable. If they weren't, they wouldn't be tempting!

Does that mean there's to be no pleasure for those who want to obey God? Far from it. It is God, in fact—not Satan—who "richly provides us with everything for our enjoyment" (1 Timothy 6:17). God is a loving father, and like any good father, he wants his children to be obedient, upright—and happy. Using the senses he gave us to enjoy the many things he has created is part of that happiness. And like any good father, God also doesn't want his children to love their pleasure more than they love him. In 2 Timothy 3:2-4, he even says that, in the last days, men will turn from God because they will be "lovers of pleasure rather than lovers of God."

It's a choice you make. Either God or pleasure has to be on top. One or the other. They can't both rule your life.

There's nothing wrong with pleasure. Enjoy your God-given senses, within the standards of behavior God gave us in the Bible.

But what will you love more? God? Or pleasure?

VERSE OF THE DAY:

For the grace of God that brings salvation has appeared to all men. It teaches us to say "No" to ungodliness and worldly passions, and to live self-controlled, upright, and godly lives in this present age. —Titus 2:11, 12

Then Jesus said to his disciples, "If anyone would come after me, he must deny himself and take up his cross and follow me." —*Matthew 16:24*

HEY!
That passage in 2 Timothy we quoted part of earlier really shows you what kind of company "lovers of pleasure" keep. Read it now: 2 Timothy 3:2-4.

JUST DO IT:
You've seen what the Pleasure Principle is; it's quoted above. Now take a look at today's verses, along with the rest of the verses quoted in today's reading, and come up a new principle of your own. A principle that describes how we as Christians can appropriately respond to the many choices that face us each day. Call it the Jesus Principle.

But make sure this principle doesn't exclude any thought of pleasure or happiness for us. God wants us to enjoy our senses. He just doesn't want that enjoyment—rather than obedience to him—to rule our lives.

GETTING WASTED

When I was in high school, one of my friends decided to drink a whole six-pack of beer by himself.

And he did—but he didn't keep it down long. First, he threw up until there was nothing left in his stomach. Then, while he cried for his mommy, he tried to throw up some more, but there was nothing left to come out. He was trying so hard, I expected to see his tennis shoes come flying out.

Two days later, in the locker room, with a group of admiring kids gathered around, the same guy was boasting, "Man, did I get wasted Saturday night! I drank at least a whole six-pack, maybe more. I don't even remember half the stuff I did that night, but I remember it was great! What a riot! I was really bombed."

Throwing up is great? A riot? I wasn't the world's most experienced individual at that age, but I knew enough to know that was nonsense. If painful dry heaves is a great time, then why waste money on the beer? Just sneak off to a private place and stick your finger down your throat. Or sip a raw egg through a straw.

That was a bunch of years ago, but somehow too many people—especially teenagers—still think that getting wasted is fun. A poll of high-school kids taken a year ago asked them first what words they think their parents would associate with a fun party. The kids answered with words like: *cocktails, dancing, cards, conversation, food*. Then the poll asked the kids what words *they* would associate with a fun party. The answers were a bit different: *wasted, drunk, booze, drugs, passed out, bombed, sex*. Reminds me of my friend throwing up his tennis shoes.

You don't have to buy that lie just because somebody bragging in a locker room says it's true. I've been spending a great deal of time lately with kids who had been alcoholic or addicted to drugs but have now been through a treatment program and are clean. Almost without exception, even though they sometimes miss being high, they feel as though they have their life back again, the life that drugs and alcohol had taken away from them. They're trying hard not to go back to where they were. They've tried both, and they know that sobriety is better. And more fun.

"Getting wasted" is a waste. Stay straight.

VERSE OF THE DAY:

Do not join those who drink too much wine
or gorge themselves on meat,
for drunkards and gluttons become poor,
and drowsiness clothes them in rags.

—*Proverbs 23:20, 21*

HEY!

So how should we behave, if getting wasted is out? Read Romans 13:12-14.

JUST DO IT:

Take your own "getting wasted" poll. What words do you think of when you think of having a good time? Make a list of ten words. Be honest.

If your list consists mostly of potentially destructive words like *wasted, bombed, drunk, drugs, booze,* and *passed out,* then it's time for an attitude adjustment, because it sounds like you've bought the lie. And you could be headed for a destructive lifestyle that, once you're in, you can't easily get out of. Talk it over with a trusted adult friend.

A FAIRY TALE— FOR REAL

*O*nce there was a great and wise king whose kingdom had been at war with a neighboring nation for as long as anyone could remember.

"O great king, live forever," said his general one day after limping into the throne room and kneeling.

"What is the report of the battle?" the king asked anxiously.

"We have been pushed back on all fronts," the general replied sadly, "and every day more reinforcements pour in from the enemy's lands. My soldiers are downhearted; many are injured. There is grumbling. Some—" He hesitated. "Some have even deserted and joined the enemy. The battle goes poorly."

The king sat long in thought, chin resting on his hands. At last he spoke: "Then my son shall join the battle."

The general looked up in surprise, eyes lit now with hope. "Yes! Perhaps the prince in white raiment, riding a white stallion!"

But the king shook his head. "His time for white raiment will come. But now the soldiers need no prince in white raiment. Now they need someone to teach them how to be common soldiers, in faithfulness and humility."

"And so I shall, my father, if it be your will," said the prince, entering the throne room and removing his crown.

And so he did. He wore the uniform of a soldier, he lived in the mud with the soldiers, and he ate poor food and slept in rough blankets on the hard ground. Indeed, though it was rumored that the new soldier among them was the prince of the land, few soldiers believed it.

But all of them noticed that he did not grumble or complain about the soldier's life or the dangers of war. He was quick to smile and even to laugh, he was easy to talk to, and offered his friendship to all around him. Slowly, the attitudes of the soldiers changed. Those who had been discouraged and ready to slip away found new hope and stayed. The ill and wounded healed quickly and returned to their posts. In battle, the king's soldiers fought with a new fierceness; their weapons gleamed in the sun. Someone had shown them how to be soldiers.

The army of the enemy, accustomed to easy victories, grew silent and exchanged worried glances. Soon the final battle began. And at its end, it was the brave soldiers of the king, exhausted but victorious, who raised their swords in a glad song of triumph—until someone pointed out, broken and bloody on the field of battle, the body of the new soldier who had inspired their victory: the prince.

But with the sound of trumpets, onto the battlefield rode the king himself in a chariot of gold, and he leaped down and gathered his son in his arms. The king carried the prince to a brook nearby, and bathed his wounds, and dressed his body in white raiment, and then breathed on his face—once, twice, and at the third breath the prince's eyes opened, and he sat up.

Then the soldiers cheered, and they gathered stones and built a great mound and brought the prince's throne from the palace and placed it there high and lifted up, and sat the prince upon it, and worshiped him.

Does that story sound familiar? It should—it's the story told over and over again in the Bible—in Philippians 2:5-11, for instance: Jesus voluntarily humbling himself, Jesus submitting to an agonizing and humiliating death, and Jesus raised again and exalted and given "the name that is above every name, that at the name of Jesus every knee should bow."

What an encouragement that should be to any of his followers, such as you and me, who've ever been ignored or made fun of because we're Christians, or who've felt like it's all the other people—the ones not restricted by Christianity—who have all the fun. Relax! Every knee will bow to him. Every tongue will admit that Jesus Christ is Lord. Our guy wins.

Too often we allow ourselves to feel like losers. But we serve the Supreme Winner of all time. And his victory, which he'll share with us, will be complete and final and more public and worldwide than TV! (Remember—*every* tongue and *every* knee!)

Friends may desert you, your family may cause you great pain, and you may suffer disappointments in other areas. But through all of that, let's never lose sight of the majesty of Christ, the one who taught us by his example how to be soldiers.

VERSE OF THE DAY:

Therefore God exalted him to the highest place
*   and gave him the name that is above every name,*
that at the name of Jesus every knee should bow,
*   in heaven and on earth and under the earth,*
and every tongue confess that Jesus Christ is Lord,
*   to the glory of God the Father.*

—Philippians 2:9-11

HEY!

If Jesus is that mighty and majestic, how should we respond to him with our lives?
Read Philippians 3:10-14.

JUST DO IT:

Keep the "fairy tale" that started today's reading in mind as you go through your day. You don't need to be intimidated by the people around you who obviously don't believe as you do, who live as if there is no God, who speak and act in ways that don't please him. You don't have to feel outnumbered when you're surrounded by an unbelieving world. God hasn't given up on those people yet; many of them will still come to him. And in the end, God will still be in control of the world he created. You're on the winning side.

Remember that today.